Who's That Clown at My Desk?

Who's That Clown at My Desk?

William A. Weimer

iUniverse, Inc.

New York Lincoln Shanghai

Who's That Clown at My Desk?

iUniverse books may be ordered through booksellers or by contacting:

iUniverse
2021 Pine Lake Road, Suite 100
Lincoln, NE 68512
www.iuniverse.com
1-800-Authors (1-800-288-4677)

© *William A. Weimer, 2005*
Asheville, North Carolina

ISBN-13: 978-0-595-36868-6 (pbk)
ISBN-13: 978-0-595-81279-0 (ebk)
ISBN-10: 0-595-36868-9 (pbk)
ISBN-10: 0-595-81279-1 (ebk)

Printed in the United States of America

Contents

Preface

As soon as early humans began to organize activities into teams of workers, four key roles began to emerge. These were the king, the warrior, the shaman, and the fool, each of which played a role essential to the survival of the tribe. As we evolved to today's highly complex organizations, the four roles continued to be essential for success. However, in many of our organizations, the roles are no longer in balance. For example, many of our workplaces are becoming increasingly bureaucratic and less fun for workers. Some organizations are driven by narcissistic and greedy managers who exercise their (usually) male egos in top-down direction setting, too often called "leadership" by management consultants. The supply of shamans and fools, or, as they are called in this book, priests and clowns—is dwindling. Many organizations have reached a point at which top managers no longer tolerate advice on right and wrong by thoughtful priest role players; nor are some managers willing to accept court jesters, or clowns, as they play their needed roles in challenging authority.

This is a book about teams and teamwork. Teams are not just managers and workers, or kings and warriors. They are groups of people, all with objectives to accomplish specific work goals. To do that usually requires more than leadership and followership. This book is about the roles that are necessary for success as teams try to meet their work objectives. It is about the roles that are played by various team members as they work to meet their goals. Based on observation, the roles needed for success are identified and described. Kings and warriors are the obvious roles. Not so obvious are the priest and clown roles, yet they are also quite necessary for teams to function successfully.

This book describes those four roles and then points out that two of them are declining in number and already in short supply. That is the problem: there are not enough people playing the roles of priest and clown. What is needed are people who are secure enough in their jobs to take on these two roles and fill in what we are missing. If you can play either of these roles, this book provides your new and additional job description.

Do you believe that your work organization is perfect? If not, are you willing to do something to improve it? If you are willing to work to improve the effectiveness of your organization, this is the book for you. You should read this book if you are willing to make recommendations, become a whistle-blower if necessary, or start a movement for improvement within your organization. If this sounds risky, that's because it is. To handle the risk involved, you will need to be fairly secure in your job. Perhaps you are regarded as a long-term employee, of value to your company or organization and therefore more secure than most. Perhaps you are independently wealthy and don't need your job in order to feed your family. Perhaps you are secure enough to be willing to take some risk to improve your organization and are not especially concerned about being fired or "down-sized" for becoming an occasional corporate irritant. If you fit one of these descriptions, you are potentially part of a much-needed work force—and you are one of the people to whom this book is addressed.

Of course, anyone is free to read the book. It will be useful to human resources people. It may be useful to consultants in the relatively new field of modern organizational anthropology. It will provide insight to anyone in the process of changing jobs and organizations, by providing a new way to "see" the contrast between the old workplace and the new one. Even a manager or two, among the few who read books, may find it helpful as they try to improve their organizations and workplaces.

The stories in this book are based on actual events, people, and roles played. The names of individuals have been changed and the facts altered only to the extent necessary to protect both the innocent and the guilty from any embarrassment. It is therefore purely coincidental if any of these events appears to match your real-life experience.

The author has forty years of experience in managing technology-based projects in industry, where he became an observer and critic of the corporate scene. As a result of some of his observations, he has been occasionally labeled a "corporate irritant." He has previously published two books containing more of his observations:

- *Masters and Patrons: Renaissance Solutions for Today's Productivity Problems* (Marietta, GA: Dogwood Publishing Company, 1992).

- *Learning to Manage in a Complex Organization* (Enschede, The Netherlands: Twente University Press, 1999).

Acknowledgments

At first, I thought the subject of this book was an original idea. Perhaps it was as it is presented here, but when I began looking into basic roles played in projects and in human society generally, I found several references that support my theories and contributed to my thinking as I wrote the final draft.

The first is *The Hunters*, an award winning documentary film made in 1957 by John Marshall. The historian William Irwin Thompson, describes it in a book, *The Edge of History* (1971). In the film, four bushmen of a South African tribe set out to search for food. The four are quite different in their behavior, their thinking patterns, and their methods of attacking and resolving problems. The first is the *headman*, the group's leader. He is the decision maker and direction setter. He provides the group with stability and structure. The second is the *warrior*, or hunter, a strong, athletic man. Third is the *shaman*, a dreamer and seer of visions, the group's reader of signs and omens. The fourth man is the *clown*. He entertains children the group meets along the way. He understands both people and animals and has the ability to strip away masks and reveal truth.

Thompson suggests that "the film is also poetically eloquent in presenting in high relief the structure of a primary human group." Thompson's book confirmed my belief that there were indeed four fundamental roles being played in successful modern organizations. However, I deviated from his conclusion that the shaman is today the inventor, and the clown the entrepreneur.

In 1986, psychologist Ben Romine wrote a paper, as yet unpublished, entitled, *From Stone Age Bands to Modern Leadership: A New Way to Look at Organizations*. Referring to the work of Thompson, Romine first points out that the headman and warrior are rational and operational in their way of approaching their work, while the shaman and clown are more intuitive and ideational in their outlook. He points out that each of the four at times plays mentor to each of the others. He read and commented on two of the drafts of this book. Several discussions with Mr. Romine convinced me that the general idea of the four roles as presented in this book might provide help in understanding modern industrial organizations. His support and encouragement are much appreciated.

My search turned up much in the way of references to the clown role. Manfred F. R. Kets de Vries's book *Leaders, Fools, and Impostors: Essays on the Psychol-*

ogy of Leadership (2003) is essential reading for anyone wishing to explore further the role of the clown, or fool. The book confirmed my observations of clowns that I had known in organizations, and it provided further insight into this role, which is needed to help deal with our kings' diseases of the ego.

My thanks to several who read and commented on an early draft of this book. Phil Dutton, Marge and Darrel Lauer, Bob McGarrah, Jim Richards, Roy Klaskin, and Viktors Berstis all made comments that led to substantive changes in my approach to the subject. My thanks to all of them for their assistance. Robert van der Ven, Menno Huson, and Arjen van Dijk have been discussing the priest and clown roles with me for several years. They too made helpful comments that are much appreciated.

My wife, Julie, made many helpful comments as the work went along. She played the clown role to my ego as well as the priest role when it came to giving me advice. She will not believe it, but the roles she played were very much appreciated in this project.

Finally, a sincere thank you to my publisher, iUniverse. Publishing Services Assistant, Jon D. McWilliams became my contact with the firm. He managed the process of getting this book published. There undoubtedly were others involved, but Jon provided for all my contact with the firm. My editor at iUniverse, David Bernardi, gets much credit for smoothing out my mishandling of the English language and for his very helpful suggestions for improvement throughout the book. Jon and David made it a pleasure for me to work with iUniverse.

1

Four Tales from Industry

All the world's a stage,
And all the men and women merely players;
They have their exits and their entrances;
And one man in his time plays many parts....

—Shakespeare, *As You Like It,* act II, scene vii.

Dave's Bird

Dave is a master at the art of software development. He works crazy hours and writes computer software that is as close to error free as anyone in the industry. About twenty years ago, he was working on a project that required him to use the large central computer system as he developed a program for a personal computer. Picture him using his terminal for a short period and then shifting to the PC for a time and then back again to the terminal. The rhythm of his work followed this pattern for several months.

One day, the person managing the large central computing system decided that he could save computer time and allow more users to connect if they "timed out" any user who did not enter anything for a period of five minutes. When this was announced to all users, Dave could see that he would have a problem with such an arrangement. He knew that many of the periods when he was using only his PC were longer than five minutes. He called the computer center manager and described his problem with the five-minute time-out decision, but nothing was done to change the decision or to accommodate Dave's needs. As a good soldier, Dave felt he had to accept the decision without argument.

A creative person, Dave began to think of ways to circumvent the problem. He realized that all he really needed was some way to strike a terminal key at least every four minutes and fifty-nine seconds. One day as he was passing through a novelty shop he saw the answer. It was a small plastic bird that would tilt down to "drink" every minute or so. He decided to build one for himself.

With a few parts, including a timer and small battery, he constructed a "bird" that would stand on his terminal keyboard and, every four minutes and fifty seconds, tilt down and "peck" the enter key. The problem was solved!

At the time, Dr. Bob W. was the manager of another department, with no official connection to Dave and his work. When Bob heard the story and saw the bird, he asked Dave to take a photo of it. Bob then sent the photo and a note to the manager of the computer center, describing the problem and stating that if the decision to "time off" the users not striking a key within five minutes was not reversed, or at least modified to meet Dave's needs, Bob would see to it that the story and photo would appear on every bulletin board in the building. He stated that the heading would be "Our Computer Service." Within one day, the decision was reversed.

Who are these people in our story? In our work in organizations, we often hear descriptive names for roles we see being played. Some examples are "old warrior," "crown prince," "Rabbi," "good soldier," "work horse," "the king," "clown," "pretender to the throne," "the power behind the throne," "high priest," "boy king," and many others.

Dave, the master programmer, is clearly the worker in the drama. He's the warrior, the good soldier, marching forward with his work and finding creative solutions to problems he encounters along the way. Perhaps the word "warrior" best describes the role Dave plays. The word "master" further specifies that he is not just any warrior but one with special skills who performs highly specialized tasks.

The manager of the computing department plays a clear role as well. He is one with power to make decisions that affect the work of others. He may have the power to hire and fire workers, at least within the computer center. Let's think of him as playing the role of a monarch, or king, in our story.

Finally, what kind of clown would send the note with the photograph to the manager? The word "clown" is as good a description as any for Bob's role here. Why clown? The clown (in the old days, the court jester) was the person who could tell the king things he didn't want to hear. These days, the industrial clown is probably viewed as a corporate irritant. That's also a fair description of the role Bob was playing, but at least he was an irritant with the motivation to help improve the situation.

"Mid-Mortem" Reviews?

A manager of a small software development department decided that a review would be useful about midway through a project. She thought of it as a "mid-mortem" review, as opposed to the usual "post-mortem" review that was normally held after all the work on a project was completed. She was quite certain that it should be conducted "off site" and that lunch should be part of what she had planned as a four-hour meeting. She made plans for the topics to be discussed as well as problems and issues to be covered. Then she went to her manager for approval.

She quickly learned that "the guidelines" did not permit off-site meetings of any kind; she further learned that the firm paying for lunch was out of the question. Undeterred, the manager went to one of her advisor friends and discussed what she wanted to do and how to get around "the guidelines." The result? The meeting was held—in a church. Everyone brought a sack lunch and the manager paid for the coffee and soft drinks out of her own pocket.

The review was a success, and what it accomplished in the way of increased motivation found its way into the hearing of higher levels of management. The term "mid-mortem" became a popular code word in that organization for doing certain things "outside the guidelines." Higher level managers, too, learned from the example.

Holding a business meeting in a church is perhaps a bit unusual. However, churches offer unused space during much of the workweek, and most may be willing to offer a place for a meeting for a small donation. In the example of the "mid-mortem" review, the manager offered to make a donation, but her group took up a small collection to solve that problem. Obviously, the event had become a sort of family-style affair—after a bit of bureaucracy had nearly stopped it. Long after the event, workers in that organization reflected that it was one of the more successful, fun meetings they had attended while at work.

In this example, the manager and her manager play king roles. The workers are the warriors. The warriors were quite involved in the process; they even donated the "cost" of the meeting space. There is a mentor or advisor who provides advice; we might think of him as one who plays a kind of priest role.

"The Worst Product…"

Here's still another programmer story. This one took place many years ago, during the computer age "BT," or "Before Terminals." Only large, complex computers were in use then. Programming was, in those days, regarded as an art, practiced by people with strange appearances and even stranger ways of thinking.

This little drama took place in a software development center. The staff included about one hundred programmers, plus the various support personnel: computer operators, secretaries, technical writers, and others.

One day, the center manager received a phone call from the assistant to the president of the division in which he worked. It was to inform him that a customer, who was experiencing some problems with one of the center's products, had come upon an error message that stated, "This is the worst product this company has ever made." The center manager was told to track down the programmer who had done this terrible deed and fire him or her. He responded that that might be difficult, since there were more than one hundred people in the center and since the message could have been produced by any of them.

We might ask, "What clown could have done such a stupid thing?" In this case, we are not considering a helpful court jester; we are considering a person who did a stupid thing—yes, it probably was done with wry humor, or on a day when nothing was going well, but it was a foolish thing to have done nevertheless. Perhaps this clown was truly a fool.

Humor is often viewed by managers somewhat differently than by workers.

The center manager's problem was that, of the one hundred programmers, he immediately thought he knew who had done it. His "suspect" was generally a free spirit—and a very good programmer. He had worked on the product in question and he had had to work long hours to meet the planned release date for the product. He could have easily become a bit disenchanted with his work more than once during the development of the product.

By the time two days had elapsed, the manager was still "thinking" about what to do. By then, he had received a letter from the division president, firmly stating what the assistant had said during the phone call. E-mail had not yet appeared on the scene, so this kind of thing was often carefully documented by letter.

What happened to the programmer? The manager never did learn with certainty the identity of the culprit—nor did he try to do so. He presented a story to top management about the complexities involved, the numbers of programmers to be considered, and the various test groups that were involved in assuring the quality of the product. Even a member of a test group could have inserted the offending sentence.

Still, the manager felt that he had to take some sort of disciplinary action. Although his "suspect" was a good programmer, something had to be done to make certain that he understood the risks he was taking in playing the fool. The manager called him in for a short meeting; just the two of them were present, the programmer's immediate manager having been excluded. The center manager showed the programmer the letter and stated that he could not determine exactly who had done such damage to the center's product. He said that he knew that the programmer could have done it, but he did not want a confession. He simply stated that he had replied to top management that he could not identify the person. He further stated that what he really wanted was a working programmer, one who worked really well—and that's exactly what he got from this particular programmer for years into the future.

Again, the roles are interesting. The programmer was a very good worker (at least most of the time), the warrior in the drama. There were two people playing king roles, the division president and the center manager, a less important king. The assistant may have been another warrior. Note that the center manager's role was not that of king throughout the entire process. He also played a sort of priest or advisor role, trying to do what was right—right for the worker, right for the product center, and right for the firm.

A Magnificent Salesman

George was managing director of the Balkan Institute of Technology. In 1995, it was an association of firms   some local, some international—for the purpose of sharing resources to perform research in the field of textiles. New types of looms, new dyeing technology, and the development of synthetic fabrics were some of the potential topics for research projects. The firms paid membership fees that totaled to a bit more than the overhead costs, the extra money to go toward preliminary work needed to identify topics as candidates for research projects. Then, when specific projects were agreed upon, the firms interested in sharing the results would put up additional funds. The organization had a board of directors made up of representatives of the member firms.

George was the boss; most of the staff thought of him as "King George." He was always on top of things. He knew people at each member firm. He had had some training in engineering and science, but he was best at being the front man; he was a super salesman. He was aristocratic in his conduct, and he was more than a bit overweight, all of which added to his charisma, his "presence." He was truly magnificent.

The organization was a relatively small one when George became its boss. In addition to himself, he had an assistant, plus an occasional person from one of the member companies whom he borrowed to do some of the preliminary work in identifying projects. The organization ran smoothly until the board of directors decided to add an education function. The objective of this addition was to create a master's degree program in technology management, with concentration on the technology being studied and on managing technology-based projects in industry. As a result of the change, the organization grew to ten people, including a manager of the education project, three faculty members, an admissions manager, a librarian, and two assistants.

The board of directors had quickly agreed to provide for the startup costs of the education project. Based in Balkan countries, most of the firms urgently needed to improve their understanding of the Western capitalist way of doing business, the profit motive and business practices of the West, and their expectations of Western businesses regarding international free trade, in particular, free trade in textiles.

At the beginning, the organization functioned well. The people on the staff liked and respected one another. Very quickly, a strong commitment to cooperation developed. Norman, the education project manager, was a quiet, serious, somewhat introspective man, who had developed the preliminary plans for the master's degree project.

The organization leased new working space, with offices, a classroom, and a space for a small library. George decided that he should have his office in the same general area, so they added space for him and his secretary. His office was to be special, requiring more than the usual office area to accommodate one person. He argued that this was necessary to help him attract new members and to impress potential students.

The design work on the curriculum had begun in January. It was to be ready for a small group of twelve "experimental" students by September. Qualified visiting lecturers were identified and scheduled. During the first few months that Norman, the education manager, was in charge of this activity, all proceeded according to plan. However, once George had moved into his new office, strains began to appear in some of the working relationships. George demanded regular reviews of the project, and during the reviews he would frequently overrule his education manager on issues relating to the course design. George encouraged everyone on the staff to come directly to him with questions and problems, often failing to involve Norman in the discussions or decisions.

Once the course had begun, George would frequently demand "an hour to talk with the students." These at first seemed to form a kind of management seminar on the ways of Western business, and the students found them valuable.

However, soon after the first two of these lectures, students began to complain that what they were getting was propaganda, not unlike what they had heard during their years under Communism. George soon heard some of the students' views; his reaction was to place a sign outside his office in the corridor leading to the library and classroom. The sign read, "No students beyond this point."

That is perhaps sufficient to introduce George, Norman, and the staff. You can easily imagine some of the other incidents in the story. It's an example of what all too often is an imperfect beginning of a business venture with sound potential.

Some of the players in the drama and the roles they played are easy to identify. There is King George, the magnificent. There is Norman, the quiet, competent planner. We'll need a name for his role; many organizations have their Normans as they develop; perhaps *philosopher* or *priest* would not be too far off the mark. Of course, there were the other staff people, workers, and, we can assume, good soldiers in the project; they were the warriors. One role was clearly missing, however: that of the clown. There was no one playing the court jester to King George, and he frequently needed someone to show him the effect of his actions.

Teamwork?

In these four stories, we have identified four roles played by people working in organizations. The roles appear wherever we find people working in teams to produce a result. We have begun to name the roles based largely on appearances—and perhaps too little data. Clearly there is the warrior role—the worker who marches ahead to accomplish the task. Some of the warriors we meet are masters of their trade; some are not. It seems that there are warriors in every work project, good soldiers who march forward to carry out the objectives of the organization and the project.

Another role, obvious in all the stories is the king role. Yes, we call them managers in industry, administrators in schools and hospitals, but they have the power to make decisions that affect people, plans, budgets, and the functioning of entire organizations. The word "king" may be the shortest, most descriptive name for this role. As we think about the king in the "King George" story, we may have also realized something about ego and power, possibly the abuse of power; that too may be sometimes related to the king role.

In addition to the warrior and king roles that appear in all teams and all projects, we have identified two other roles, clown and priest, a bit less obvious than king and warrior. The priest, if that is a reasonable name for the role, appears as a quiet, principled, sometimes introverted person. He is often associated with planning, or at least thinking about the future of some project or organization. Sometimes he is also a teacher, advisor, or mentor.

The clown role is easier to identify when someone chooses to play it. He is the court jester who challenges the authority figure. He performs a role of somewhat greater risk as he goes about his tasks.

There appears to be another factor relating to all four of the roles as they were described here. That is that individuals may not always play a single role one hundred percent of the time. Apparently, for example, a king can function as a clown or priest at times. There are warriors who play the priest role at times. There are people who play both clown and priest, as they continue to play their warrior roles. This means that the roles are not full-time jobs; they are what we choose to play based on each individual situation.

Finally, the roles appear mostly male as they are described here and later in this book. It's true that, as early humans on our planet organized teams to address their needs, men usually played these four roles. Our modern organizations, descended from military organizations, still reflect some military male dominance. What is right, and what is wrong with our modern organizations both probably descend from their male history. It is the history and how we can improve what has been given us by that history that we are attempting to better understand.

2

The Warrior

All of us are trained to be warriors, right from the beginning, in childhood. We are taught to follow a leader, to accept the authority of our fathers and mothers, teachers, and police officers, and to accept and obey rules. We attend school, a society of authority figures, rules, and behavior modification. As we grow up, we are reminded to march in step, stay in line, obey the rules, and do a good job—in short: be a good soldier.

The others we meet along the way are mostly warriors, plus a relatively small number of kings, who are playing authority figure roles as we grow up and mature. Most our age are other warriors. Occasionally we see a priest, a real one; rarely do we see a clown, except at the circus. Therefore, if we do not adapt well to either warrior or king as our future role model, our only available option is to reject what we see. This usually means dropping out of school, or stepping outside the bounds of accepted social practices—possibly entering a life of crime.

The role of warrior is usually full time, or nearly so; it's the role that most closely matches the job. Whether farming, painting automobiles, machining parts, baking bread, or writing software, with the exception of executives heading very large organizations, this is the one of the four roles for which the person in the role is paid a full-time salary to do what the job requires: produce, achieve, and be a good soldier. Yes, a warrior may also play a priest or clown occasionally, but that is usually part time and not related directly to his job description or specific task objective.

Warriors in Organizations

The warrior is an obvious role in all organizations. The warrior is highly action oriented, has the skills to do the job, and does it with high energy. Ideally, he keeps his skills current and is always prepared to do battle for his leader, the king. He is a rational-thinking, operationally oriented person. He is an implementer;

he loves to make things happen. While small organizations require only one king, they usually grow by adding warriors.

The warrior strives to be professional in his actions and in representing his organization. He knows the work, its demands and processes. He frequently sharpens his skills; he is motivated to be "the best" at what he does. He may have the view "if you want something done right, you must do it yourself." In other words, he may be a perfectionist, because he knows that becoming successful requires it.

The warrior wants to be noted for accomplishments in his field, for his ability to deal with sudden changes and unexpected demands. His focus is on action; that means that occasionally he will break some of the rules to achieve the group's objective, which he has come to perceive as his own.

Some warriors are content to remain in this role for a lifetime of work. We should respect such decisions; yet, many managers do not understand or accept a warrior's decision to "remain" at the working level and not become a manager. Many mistakes are made, especially in high technology work today, in promoting the best scientist, engineer, or computer programmer to manager. The result too often is the loss of an excellent engineer *and* the appointment of a low-quality manager. We should avoid the temptation to make simple rules from such thoughts. It is not always true that all good workers make good managers. Nor, for that matter, is it always true that a good manager must be a king-type person. Organizations today have many team leaders and managers who are warriors in style; these jobs provide avenues of advancement for warriors wanting to play just a bit of the king role but remain in their professional work.

Many warriors do have higher goals; some aspire to become the kings of their own organizations. Some play the other three roles as needed. Most enjoy finding and performing various types of work that call for rational thinking and an operational outlook.

"Promotion" to Management

Our organizational cultures, made up mostly of people playing the roles of kings and warriors, usually develop reward systems and expectations based on the word "promotion." Often, managers and administrators think that if one is an excellent warrior, the best perhaps, he should be promoted; often, the word promotion implies advancing to management. What if the warrior doesn't want a management job? "He's crazy," is the view of the boss. "Of course he should be a manager. He's an excellent warrior." What if the warrior is not qualified to manage? "Of course he's qualified," says the boss, "he's an excellent warrior." Unfortunately, this limited view represents the practice in many, if not most, organizations. A few companies have adopted "dual career ladders" to address this problem. Many of their managers "know" that only a person of lesser accomplishment would elect to follow the "non management" ladder. In many organizations, there is not even another name for the "non management" career path.

An Educator

Edward is an educator, a master teacher, in fact. He's remembered by his students as one of the best teachers they ever had. After several years of teaching, he had reached the top of the salary scale for his particular teaching job. About the same time, he began to think seriously about his future. He talked about it with a few trusted friends, fellow teachers, and his principal. The principal decided that a promotion was the next step—after all, he would not want to lose one of the best teachers in the school system.

The promotion was, naturally, to the position of assistant principal, the first rung of the administrative ladder. In schools, it is the administrators who play the king role. The new job involved no teaching at all; instead, it involved "dealing with" children who misbehaved in school, scheduling the school buses, and preparing the classroom schedules each spring and fall. Of course, he was paid a slightly higher salary.

With a job in which he could no longer teach, Edward quickly became disenchanted with his work and the system in which he worked. He resigned and took a job with a large company for three years, and then he went to work at a university. There he could teach once again; life again was good.

A Sales Executive

Here's another example of the same kind of organizational thinking, this time in industry.

"Why," an executive of a large sales division wanted to know, "were relatively frequent mistakes made in promoting the best sales people to management positions? The candidates are always excellent performers, with excellent sales records and high customer satisfaction." "Usually," he pointed out, "such people make excellent managers." However, when the candidate did not succeed as a manager, it was always a clear case of failure. These failures did not happen in shades of gray; they were clear failures, with the new manager failing in the most basic of management tasks. "What is wrong with our selection criteria? How can we avoid these failures?"

Not all excellent workers make excellent managers.

A likely reason for these failures is that the people who were selected to the job were master warriors, people who were professionals at the job of selling, who liked that work and built their work lives around it. They were not necessarily people who aspired to the role of king; yet they may have aspired to promotion, and if they were offered management as advancement, they accepted it and did their best to succeed at it.

A Consultant

Here's yet another example, this time from the field of management consulting.

Robert had worked for several years as a warrior in industry. He became an expert in several of the more exotic management consulting areas, such as corporate mergers and acquisitions. Though he himself had never worked as a manager, he was highly successful providing consulting services to managers. He became much sought after and eventually had more business than he could handle. The obvious solution: start a consulting firm.

He hired an assistant who also worked as secretary when needed. He then hired two professionals he knew and who had already consulted in related fields. With four people in the firm, Robert still saw himself as a professional consultant, with the management of the firm something he and his assistant could handle as a secondary activity. The firm continued to be successful and continued to grow.

By the time the firm reached eight people, Robert was having some doubts about his ability to carry both of his professions—management and consultant—or, in our words, to play both the king and warrior roles. In short, the management work was taking too much time and was beginning to interfere with his consulting, the work Robert saw as his "real work." The basic decision facing him: was he naturally a king or a warrior? This isn't to say that the two roles are mutually exclusive, but he knew he would soon have to choose one for his primary work effort.

Robert knew himself well enough to know that he was a better warrior than king. He also knew that his greatest joys came when he, as a consultant, offered solutions that firms then implemented successfully. As just another small company manager, he could see that he would lose what he valued most in his work—the satisfaction of doing something himself that works! Robert decided to disband his firm. He kept his assistant and helped the others find new jobs. In most cases, they simply continued with work they were already doing, but separate from Robert's firm. A few of them established their own firms.

A Product Developer

Sharon headed a group of seven researchers, including herself. She worked as a warrior, mostly. She saw her role in management as that of team leader. She learned to handle the management tasks in as little time as possible, she did her best to remain invisible to the management structure above her, and she always avoided bureaucratic processes.

Sharon and her group had begun work on some new technologies. They made several discoveries that would justify much greater corporate investment in what they were doing. Sharon herself had realized that, but she refused to develop a proposal requesting additional workers and resources. She chose to document her group's findings in journals and said that anyone wanting to carry the work forward was free to do so.

"I have been in this product development business for more than twenty years," she said. "I know that the group of seven of us is not very likely to get much notice in this large product development laboratory. I like the work. I also have learned that eight people, or a few more, would make this 'a department,' bringing with it bureaucracy, budgets, plans, and all the rest that goes along with becoming a department. I would have to become a manager; that would interfere with my work. No, seven is the upper limit. The seven of us will continue to more than justify our existence and continue to do good work."

By now, the warrior point of view must be clear. In the choice between warrior and king, Sharon knew she was a warrior—and she was a good one.

Finally, Michelangelo

"And further, if I am to do any work for Your Holiness, I beg that none may be set in authority over me in matters touching my art. I beg that full trust may be placed in me and that I may be given a free hand." Michelangelo, the sculptor, made this statement in 1524 to the pope.

Michelangelo was asking that he be free to do his work without having to take orders from someone less qualified to judge his work. It's this point of view, expressed nearly five hundred years ago, that we frequently hear today. Could Michelangelo successfully make it through our system today?

How Do Warriors Advance?

Almost all hiring is aimed at finding warriors. After all, that is what is needed—someone to do a specific job, to follow instructions, and to be trained for the job. Nearly all of us begin our organizational lives as warriors. That means that the other roles are developed as the warriors go along in their working and organizational lives.

The idea of advancement, or moving up, is perhaps slightly more prevalent in sales and in professional work than it is on the assembly line or the shop floor. Yet, today, people from all types of employment are changing jobs and firms in increasing numbers. Few of our warriors are immune to the call of more pay, a better title, more power to make their own decisions, or, simply, "advancing" upward.

Most warriors express one of two views on their advancement possibilities. First, there are those who like the warrior job and want to keep it. These include warriors from all fields of work: from science to plumbing, from astronaut to carpenter. These warriors do not want other issues to bother with, such as meetings, budgets, management, and related subjects.

Warriors who choose to remain with their field know they will have to keep up with its new developments over time. They must grow in their field and provide leadership in it—not necessarily the leadership of the king role, but by example and the training of newly hired apprentices.

The best warriors wishing to remain in their line of work will have to learn to refuse offers of "promotion" to management or king-type jobs. Yes, when they do refuse, they will have to learn to accept that some in management will decide that they are odd people who should accept that they have done well enough to earn the reward of "advancement" to management.

Of course, warriors can change professional fields as they go along. These days, some of these changes may require additional education, perhaps a new university degree. The point is that these warriors elect to remain warriors. They like the sense of personal satisfaction that comes with doing something well.

One of the benefits of electing the warrior role is that in it one can work until nearly any age. As long as he can practice his profession and make contributions to it, he can usually continue at it. Yes, corporations have recommended retirement ages, but in most cases they are not absolute requirements. Warriors working as artists, inventors, and other professions not associated with jobs in firms are free to work as long as they are producing and keeping their knowledge and skills up to date.

Second is the warrior who wants advancement to the king role. We might think of him as the "pretender to the throne." He will require some education and personal development in management concepts and skills. This change amounts to a change in profession, not just a reward for good work as a warrior. In many organizations, the best warriors will be offered "advancement" to management or administrative—king-type—jobs. This is clearly one of the characteristics of the organizational culture in which we live and work.

Some warriors may change their minds "midstream." One may work as a warrior for a number of years and then change to the management profession, becoming a king. By then, such a person will probably be well acquainted with how organizations work and the culture of the one in which he works. Nevertheless, he should prepare himself for work in a new profession, that of management. He should also have demonstrated the ability to work with people, provide leadership, and be willing to delegate responsibility and authority to others. Delegation is often the most difficult task for a warrior to learn as he begins to occupy the king role.

Warrior Role Characteristics

Recall that the role is not necessarily the job; however, in this case the role and job may be closely related. The warrior's job is what he's paid to do, from engineering to research to accounting to brick laying, to many other professions. People holding these jobs may be warriors in their outlook; they may also be priests, clowns, or kings. For most jobs outside of management, the warrior outlook is one that usually helps the worker become successful. The person playing the warrior role can usually be described as having some combination of the following:

- action oriented

- rational and operational

- achievement oriented

- willing to obey authority and abide by rules

- a producer who identifies with the job more than the organization

- motivated to keep skills and knowledge up to date

- willing to follow the command and guidance of his leader

3

The King

The king role is needed in all organizations. A person playing this role must supply the stability and structure; he must lead and point the way. The top person—the president of the company, the managing director, or chief executive officer, often plays the role. In large organizations with many lower level managers, many jobs call for the king role to some extent.

To clarify again: the role is not the job. However, in the case of the king role, the person playing it is often an executive or administrator. At high levels in organizations, the role and the job may match closely. At lower levels of management, the person in the job will usually play the role only some of the time.

The role includes motivating the workers to accomplish the organization's goals. The king role player makes decisions along the way, sometimes after considering advice from others, and he sets the direction. He frequently needs help with his efforts to plan for the future; this often requires some of the insight of the priest, and possibly the clown, as well as the more thoughtful of the warriors. His people look to him for leadership; in fact, he sometimes occupies a father-figure role for the rest of the organization. Whether he influences it much or not, his organization, beginning when it has only a few people, becomes a kind of family. Usually, they like and respect each other and they all look to the king for protection, assistance, and leadership. It is this natural family-style organization in small companies that is most attractive to people who have previously worked in large companies that often operate mostly as bureaucracies.

As is the case with real kings in years past, and a few remaining kings today, modern organizational kings suffer from some of the same kingly diseases. Hubris, or arrogant pride, is one example. Kets De Vries (2003) says, "Hubris is a predictable offshoot of uncontrolled narcissism. Narcissism, which is a key force behind the desire for leadership and power, frequently becomes pronounced once leadership and power are attained." Power can corrupt, and it will corrupt if not for the influence of our clowns and priests.

Each of the four roles has limitations. None of the four are purely positive; all four bring positive attributes to the working organization, and all have potential liabilities, therefore all need to be considered and managed carefully. In modern management, the leadership of the king is definitely needed, but if it comes with a large measure of narcissism, his contribution to the efforts of the organization may be a small or even a negative one.

Where Do Our Kings Come From? How Are They Trained?

The king is both rational and operational in his approach to work; so, for that matter, are most of the warriors for much of the time. At times, therefore, the person playing the king role can easily shift over to that of warrior; this is particularly true in small organizations. For example, in an organization of only three, the managing director may play the king role only a small percentage of the time; for the larger portion of the available time, he plays the role of warrior. Most king role players begin as warriors, "learning the business." If they are fortunate enough to begin their king roles as heads of very small organizations, they may work at both roles for a time and then gradually assume more of the king role as their organizations grow. New kings often lack any formal training for the transition to the role.

It may come as a surprise, but managers require training to do their jobs.

A look at business school offerings provides some examples of available training for people entering or already in king roles. There are university degrees offered in business administration. There are courses in financial management, human resources management, corporate strategy development, team building, leadership, and many more. These courses, plus so-called management training courses offered by large corporations to their own new managers, represent some of the available training for the role. These courses are usually offered to people who have just been "promoted" to their first jobs as managers or who have advanced to higher executive levels. There are also short courses and seminars that, in addition to the course materials, provide participants with opportunities to discuss kingly issues with other kings in attendance. A large industry has formed around providing this type of training, sometimes called education. It has produced teaching and lecturing jobs for traveling consultants, university professors, and others.

Much of the early portion of management training is training in the "mechanics" of the job. This includes how to prepare a budget, how to produce an employee appraisal, how to delegate responsibility—in short, how to fulfill the standard requirements of the organization. In company management training courses, there may be something about the history of the firm, its primary objectives, its policies and practices, and discussions to help the new manager understand the firm's "basic values," if any have been formally stated. Most firms today have quality policies that would be included in such discussions.

Here are our rules. Follow them. Here are the procedures. Follow them. Don't make commitments without first checking with the "guidelines" and those who are charged with making sure that practices are followed. Budgets, salaries, and promotions are among the first of the practices to be understood—and followed. In other words, the art of playing the king role is learned as on-the-job training or in later courses and seminars. Here, what is referred to as the "art" of the role includes making decisions, maintaining stability, keeping order, and leading a team. What we call management training may lack much of what the king needs to play his role well.

Management training is different than what is required for an engineer, for example. Engineers, scientists, accountants, and many other warriors are trained in depth, sometimes requiring multiple university degrees. A business degree is usually viewed as helpful for sales and marketing people.

To oversimplify somewhat, our king role players are given on-the-job training. In their previous jobs in warrior roles, they learned the products, the goals, and, generally, the purpose of the company. As the best warriors, they become candidates for management positions. Some of the best become good managers; some do not. The training in the mechanics of the manager job has little to do with the success or failure of our kings. Successful kings are those who have an aptitude for working with people and who are motivated to help people succeed. The successful truly believe that their success depends on the success of their workers.

Growing with the Organization

Let's imagine a warrior who decides to start his own company. Usually the first workers are friends or warriors who have previously worked with our warrior, who wishes to play a king role in the new firm. Perhaps four or five people will make up the early organization. Our new king works only part time as king; for much of the time he is also one of the firm's working warriors. In the latter role, he is seen as a working team member.

In organizations of just a few people, most relationships are casual. Everyone knows everyone else quite well, everyone knows what the others are doing, and everyone has opinions about his own and everyone else's work. Formalizing responsibilities or formally documenting individual objectives may be done casually or not at all. It's a team, often closely knit through friendship and mutual respect. In fact, it's the mutual respect that makes the entire process of delegation a casual one, with little formality needed.

Now, let's imagine our organization after a few successful years. It may now have twenty-five people, just a few more than one person playing a king role can manage. So now there are team leaders, or first-level managers, reporting to our king. The king's job has become nearly a full-time king job, with little time left for playing warrior. Therefore, our king must change his behavior along the way. Now, while everyone knows everyone else, it may no longer be possible to retain all the casual relationships. Job descriptions, objectives, and employee appraisals must become more formal. The king may have to learn to delegate responsibility, and even authority, to his team leaders, or he may not learn this. If he does not, the enterprise will eventually fail as the king tries to "stay on top of everything" himself. The king may become dictatorial—after all, he believes it's *his* company and that he is free to do so. This will, at minimum, reduce productivity as the warriors, having lost their motivation, learn to get by with minimal work. In short, our king must change his behavior, and to some extent even his personality, or his firm will fail.

Now imagine the firm, years later, at two hundred. No longer does everyone know everyone else. The firm may be divided into "functional areas," such as sales, product development, manufacturing, and even a headquarters staff. The king must change again; now he must become an executive. To succeed, he must become more statesmanlike; he must learn to spend time and effort developing long-range plans and strategies and do so in such a way as to develop a sense of personal ownership in the other kings and warriors inside the firm.

Large organizations attempt to duplicate this learn-as-you-go growth pattern by first advancing the warrior/candidate to managing a small department; then, if successful, they advance him to a level higher, where he has managers reporting to him. Failure is not quite as costly to the large firm as it was to our small and growing firm. In large firms, failure is simply "managed" by moving the failing king to another job, perhaps a headquarters staff position from which he can view the business from a larger perspective and, with luck, learn about his errors. He may, depending on the seriousness of the failure, be moved "back" to a warrior role.

A Complex King Job

The role of the king is complex at higher levels in large organizations, complex enough to obscure some of the basic concepts of the role. Here is a look at one firm's product development executives as they carried out their kingly functions.

A few years ago, two managers in the training function of a very large corporation set out to determine what training top-level executives might need. They were quite successful with the courses they and their training group were offering, so successful that they began to think of widening the scope of training offerings. They began to think that even the kings of the organization they were serving could benefit from some training. These kings were the managing directors of the product development laboratories, each presiding over an organization of several hundred people, in some cases many more.

The two training department managers set out, practically and logically, to determine what to offer the managing directors. First, they decided to list the key skills that resulted in the best performing managing directors. Knowing ten of the twenty kings well enough to make such an evaluation, they set to work debating and listing the skills that made the very best. They then went to business textbooks and found the authors' lists of key abilities required to manage in the world of product development. The resulting list looked something like this:

- Administrator: ability to effectively deal with the corporate rules and procedures

- Technical Leader: ability to grow the technical capability of people in the organization

- Planner: ability to plan and prepare the organization for its future

- Business Manager: ability to make financial tradeoffs, produce, and achieve business plans

- People Manager: ability to develop and keep high motivation and morale

- Sales: ability to sell the company on their organization's programs and to effectively represent the organization

- General Leader: ability to focus a large group on its goals

- Executive Manager: ability to manage high-level managers

The two training managers then began their own private evaluation of the kings. They had access to the performance measures of each of the business areas, and they had their own assessment of each of the managing directors. They quickly discovered that, of the top two, in terms of long-term performance against their business objectives, each had, at most, acceptable levels of only three of these skills! They couldn't believe it. They decided that something must be wrong with the "study." A second try produced the same result: some of the kings—in fact, the best ones—were achieving excellence without the requisite number of key abilities.

The question they were forced to deal with was this: "If we have the correct list of needed abilities, and if we have correctly evaluated our managing directors, then how are they making up for the abilities they lack?"

The answer was that *other* people were supplying the missing abilities at the right times and right places in a smoothly running process. In one situation, the boss of the king (yes, in large organizations, even kings have bosses) was supplying executive management and the administrative ability. One of the people working for the king supplied the sales and planning skills. The managing director was doing an excellent job of general leadership, technical leadership, and business management. The people-management abilities needed were somehow supplied by the combination of the three.

What the two training managers never learned was whether this team arrangement was actually planned or came about by coincidence as the three people worked together. The lesson they did learn was that to be a highly successful king, you do not have to have all the necessarily abilities, but you must be able to identify your missing abilities, admit they are missing, and find a way to get others to supply them as needed in your organization.

To be fair to the king role players in the above story, look again at the list of functions the managing directors' jobs required. Not all are king role functions; some are clearly better provided by warriors, priests, and clowns. For example, the planner function is ideally suited to the long-range outlook of a person acting in the role of the priest, who provides a vision of the future. The technical leadership requirement might call for an experienced master warrior. In the same way, an experienced master sales warrior might best fill the selling requirement. Yes, there is plenty of opportunity for a clown to remind the king that he is not capable of supplying all the functions himself. What we have here in the analysis of the job of the managing director, is the requirement that all four roles must come together in a harmonious, smoothly running team relationship. The art of the king role here is to supply executive and leadership skills and to see that all the required skills are present in a smoothly functioning team, no matter which members hold which actual jobs in the organization.

A single individual, even one who believes he has all the necessary skills cannot perform many of the complex jobs in our modern corporate cultures. There are kings who have chosen to operate as dictators and believe they are infallible at providing all things to all people. However, the rest of us know they are mistaken.

No manager has all the skills that his organization needs.
That's why he has an organization.

The King's Authority

Some people believe that authority has been conferred upon them by the fact that they sit at the top of an organization. Some believe that their ownership of a firm is sufficient to give them absolute authority. Yet, that authority is not a positive motivating factor when you ask one of your warriors to perform some task. Consider what happened to Dr. Bob W., the same Dr. Bob we met in Chapter 1.

A few years ago, Bob became the manager of a group of fifty-five. He thought of himself as the organization's king, and he knew absolutely that he had the authority to get things done. One of his first problems was that several of the people did not arrive for work at or before the scheduled time. Some came in as much as an hour late. The result was reduced ability to hold meetings or do anything else that required communication between people during the first hour of the workday. Bob decided to exercise his authority and solve the problem.

He called the group's team leaders together and insisted that everyone be at work at the scheduled time, short of family emergencies, accidents, and the like. He went so far as to suggest that repeated offenders would be warned and eventually fired if they did not adhere to the work schedule. There was some discussion in the meeting about the undesirability of professionals having to punch time clocks and about truly creative people not being able to create on a nine-to-five work schedule. Bob simply repeated his position and concluded the meeting.

The situation improved somewhat, but only to a minimally acceptable level. Some continued to come in fifteen to thirty minutes late, improving only slightly after continued reminders. Clearly the offenders were seeking the point at which Bob would accept their behavior with minimum change on their part. There was grumbling, and it was beginning to infect the entire organization. The organization was beginning to adopt a "just enough to get by" view, not only related to coming to work on time but on their attitude and their job performance. Bob began to think seriously about what he had done to solve the problem and how that had not really solved it.

Bob called another meeting, this time the entire group. He lifted all requirements relating to working hours except that each person must continue to carry out the requirements of his job satisfactorily. Bob admitted that the enforced work schedules were a mistake on his part. He said that people who have interesting and challenging work to do not only come to work on time but frequently work longer than the required number of hours. Further, he said, he would devote more of his energies to providing the group with more interesting and challenging work.

The result was amazing. The tardiness problem slowly dropped off. The somewhat hostile attitude began to disappear. Morale began to improve. Bob realized that his directness in admitting his mistake had earned him greater respect and therefore a more positive attitude in responding to his future requests.

Why would a direct command using an authoritative style cause people to develop a "just enough to get by" attitude? The need to exercise authority as Bob did in the first meeting may be due to a kind of distrust of the workers; he may not have fully trusted himself either. Would a dictatorial king have this same authoritative style? Would he have the same distrust of people in his organization? Is it possible that authority conferred by a king's title, or ownership of the corporation, is a kind of negative motivator and, as such, should be used sparingly, if at all? As usual, we are left with a few questions.

Weaknesses and Imperfections

So far, we have noted a few imperfections in our selection and development of kings. Hubris, or arrogant pride, is one example. Power, as it increases, results in an increased tendency to narcissism. Power can corrupt, and it will corrupt without the active influence of our clowns and priests. Another example, related to hubris and the hunger for power, is greed. In the United States, the average executive pay in all its forms is now some five hundred times that of the average worker. The ratio is nowhere near that level in other industrialized nations. This runaway executive compensation in the United States is a direct result of greed, and it has led to public scandals relating to tax loopholes, dishonest accounting firm advisors, workers being cheated out of pensions and healthcare payments, and, finally, bankrupt firms. Even as some firms have gone bankrupt, the top executives have gone off with millions in benefits. The pay gap is one of the direct measures indicating a weakness in our organizational system's king role. This is discussed further in Chapter 6.

We have mentioned the selection and training of our organizational kings. If all that is needed is to perform well as a warrior, then what about the list of skills required to perform in the role of king, including administration, planning, business management, and the other skills mentioned earlier? Clearly, improvements can be made.

The issues relating to the skills and behavior of our kings have little to do with leadership. Yet, over the past forty years, we have had many books and courses on leadership. Some of the books were written by kings with large egos as exercises in further ego enhancement. We have consultants who advise executives on what they call "leadership styles." We have had many years of top-down management and military-style organizations, all designed with a king at the top who is supposed to lead. We have had kings who took advantage of the system and their subjects, or workers. The king role as played in many of today's organizations needs improvement. Clowns and priests may be able to help. We'll discuss their roles in the next two chapters.

King Role Characteristics

As we saw in the story about the managing directors' highly complex jobs, we must distinguish between the king role and the job a person playing the role is paid to do. With the help of those playing the other three key roles, our kings must always first ensure that all the roles are present in a smoothly running team. The person playing the king role can usually be described as some combination of the following:

- command oriented

- rational and operational

- a leader

- a decision maker

- a maintainer of stability and structure

- a parental figure at times

- committed to helping people succeed

4

The Priest

A priest in an organization tends to be quite serious, thoughtful, and interested in how and why the organization works as it does. He tends to be intuitive and ideational in his thinking. He tends to take the long view, considering trends and what the future will bring the organization as it implements a new plan. He's the organization's historian and anthropologist. You will often find him discussing the past and relating it to the present style and personality of the organization. He's a good listener and is often sought out as an advisor, particularly by younger or newer (to the organization) people who want to improve their understanding of how the organization came to be the way it is and how it works.

The modern industrial priest is the "carrier" of the organization's culture. He thinks and talks about the history, the culture, and the values of the organization, its difficult times and its great successes. Every organization has its own culture. It often forms without anyone giving much thought to what its elements should be. After many years of operation, a large organization may set to work to "plan" its mission statement, its value statements, its quality policy, and the like. In fact, these are all elements of the organization's culture, and they usually have been part of the organization to some extent since its beginning. No amount of planning or number of modern strategy sessions will change what is already there, but what is there is worth identifying, examining, and documenting.

Of course, it is possible for an organization to change. It is possible to change an organization's public image. It's possible to add a new fundamental goal or principle. For example, a firm may set out to improve its use of natural resources and improve its environmental cleanliness habits. If one of the long-term principles from its beginning had been something like "being a good corporate citizen" within the communities in which it operates, then improving its performance environmentally will easily fit in. If such a general philosophy has never been established, it will take time for the organization to develop public trust, by demonstrating through its actions that it is now serious about bettering its performance with regard to the environment. Planning and assisting with this type of organizational change is ideally suited for priests.

The priest enjoys talking about the organization *as he sees it*. Therefore, he needs access to the facts and history, perhaps even more than other workers do. Figuratively, at least, the priest sits around the campfire or evening meal with the others, offering his analysis. A priest is therefore better off if he is fully informed.

The carrier of the culture is also the person who will strengthen the moral fiber of the organization, assuming it has moral fiber to begin with. If, for example, the organization has operated with a strong sense of integrity, that is, it treats everyone inside and out with honesty, the priest will know that this is one of the company's principles, whether it has ever been stated or not, and he will promote the principle as he advises people. If the organization has a strong client service orientation, the priest will know this and will promote it at every opportunity, telling stories about "famous" customer service incidents of the past.

On the other hand, if the basic principles are not visible, or if they are left up to the individual choices of everyone in the organization, the priest will know that as well. He may approach management with recommendations relating to the principles to be followed, or he may choose to ignore the issue. He will, however, have to act if he finds conflicting principles being practiced. For example, dishonest treatment of a worker will often get a reaction from the priest, in addition to the reaction from the worker. The priest will usually not try to make a public issue of dishonesty; instead, he will quietly bring his concerns to a manager. He will usually know whether any action was taken resulting from his suggestions.

The priest role apparently grows stronger as the person playing the role ages. Older workers usually become more philosophical and know themselves better than younger workers. Perhaps this is just the wisdom that comes with age and experience. The priest's philosophical outlook, combined with his analytical capability, can become very valuable to those managing the organization. However, managers may view the priest's views as a liability, particularly if the views of the priest oppose those of the management.

As stated previously, the priest is not a full-time role in organizations. In fact, many of the priestly activities may not be done on scheduled work time at all. The person acting as a priest may also be a warrior, and as such dedicated to producing for his organization. He may be doing construction work, programming, working on an assembly line making automobiles, or working in a staff position such as human resources. He is paid to meet his work objectives, and he is evaluated on whether he does. The priest plays his role voluntarily and carries it out in addition to his regular work.

Occasionally his manager may ask for advice or his view on how certain things should be done. When this happens, he is paid, if only briefly, to play the priest role. Even more rarely will a priest have a job that *requires* priest work. There are such jobs, but there are not many, nor are they offered very often. One specific example is a staff position that was created within a human resources department in a division of a large company. The statement of work was given in one simple sentence: "Evaluate the motivational environment in…[the division] and propose change." If you are an industrial priest and are offered such a job, don't hesitate; take it.

Priests are often teachers. If you think about the role of the priest as it is described here, it's easy to see that he is a natural teacher. Therefore, one place to find some of an organization's priests would be in its training department or in human resources.

> *The priest is a carrier of the organization's culture.*
> *If the culture includes basic principles and morals,*
> *he helps to ensure they are followed.*

Finding the Priests

Give a bit of thought to identifying your organization's priests. It's not very difficult. A few questions should point the way. To whom would you go to learn the history of the organization—its unofficial history, that is, not the kind already written up in advertisements or organizational histories? To whom would you go for advice on what a recent organization change *really* means? Who do you think would offer you the best advice on planning your career in the organization (apart from your manager, of course)? Who is slightly older and more experienced and would probably be a good mentor? By now, you probably have identified two or three priests.

Now, suppose you are the manager of the organization. You might ask the same questions to help identify your priests. What should you do once you have found a priest? That's an interesting management question. A much-too-easy answer is to simply ignore the whole thing. If you discover a priest, and he is doing his work well, what difference does it make?

If you are a manager who is relatively new to the job, you will probably find that your priest offers you both edges of a sharp sword. On one hand, he would be a good advisor for you, relative to the history and values of the organization: "how we do things here." On the other hand, because of his knowledge and power—and his knowledge is power—you may see him as a threat. The decision is yours, of course. If you do decide that he's a threat, it would be best to ignore him rather than create unnecessary stress within the working group; he is probably helping to hold the group together.

What motivates a priest is somewhat different from what motivates a manager, or a king role player. The motivation of a priest is usually, first, to assist where possible. He is able to offer his services to others without expecting a return. He does not often challenge decisions; he will usually just try to understand them and include them in his picture of how the organization works—or does not work. He may not be aggressively seeking advancement; he wants to grow with his work, as we all do, but he may not especially wish to succeed his manager or to beat him out in a contest for the next higher position. He may see himself, or wish to be seen someday, as "the power behind the throne." Even that does not need to be threatening to the smooth operation of a department or firm.

As the Organization Grows

A very small or newly formed organization may not have any identifiable priests among its members. Priests, like the organization, evolve. Usually, during the time an organization grows from one to just a few people, there are no priests. The priestly advice needed, in some cases not needed, may come from the spouses of the organization's members, or from outside advisors.

An emerging priest often appears when the organization reaches fifteen or twenty members. He will usually be one of the original founding group; he will be the one who most carefully analyzed the startup and noted its problems as well as mistakes that were made. He "knew the boss when he was a younger man." This emerging priest might make a good candidate for the first human resources staff person when such a position must be filled. You should be prepared for him to "do what is right," based upon his knowledge of the organization's principles, rather than what is the most expedient.

After an organization has existed for five years, or after if it has reached fifty people or more, the role of priest should be recognizable. Whether the priests are used for their priestly services or ignored is up to the others in the organization, especially the managers. Their value can be immense or negligible; it's up to the organization and its managers.

A priest who is laid off, resigns, or is fired does not immediately become a priest in his next organization. He will require time to establish a base of knowledge in his new job. It is certain that he will identify the priests who are there and learn from them. He will emerge again in a few years and offer advice once again. Meanwhile, his loss from the old organization can be great in terms of decreasing leadership in the fostering of organizational values. On the other hand, the loss can be very small; it depends on whether his skills were used and appreciated.

Priestly Resistance

So far, priests as they are described here are content to remain in the background. They have been described as mostly nonaggressive idealists who can be ignored or employed for their extra skill and insight, as the organization desires. Do priests ever dig in their feet and resist? Yes, they do, particularly when their organization or its managers attack their views of right and wrong. Priests are usually averse to risk, unless they have a bit of the clown role in them as well. Typically, the priest will proceed carefully and logically and do his best not to offend or attack anyone directly. Nevertheless, when his organization abrogates one of its known values or acts with an obvious lack of integrity, the priest must act. He is, after all, a carrier of the moral fiber of the organization. An example will help you understand how he does this.

His manager told a worker that, as of a given date about one month in the future, his salary would be increased by five hundred dollars per month. He was happy about the increase, and he and his wife celebrated the promise. It represented a bit more than a ten percent increase in his salary.

The manager who made the statement to the worker about the salary increase had not yet cleared the amount with the salary administrator of the firm, but as he understood the rules, the amount of the raise was within "the guidelines." Upon sending the request to the salary administrator, the manager was told that the maximum amount was limited to four hundred dollars for "this employee in this situation." After a rather heated discussion with the salary administrator, the manager reported to his employee that he had made an error; the salary increase would only be four hundred dollars.

At first, the worker rationalized that an eight percent increase was nearly as good as a ten percent increase. But the whole idea that he had been promised something only to see that promise broken would not leave his mind. Finally, after realizing that the whole incident was affecting his work, he appealed to the managing director of the firm.

If you were the managing director of the firm, would you give the worker a rational explanation of the decision, recognize that a small error had been made, apologize for it, and finally tell him to go back to work, or reverse the decision of the salary administrator, give the worker the full amount as promised, and then counsel the manager who had made the promise not to do something so stupid as to make promises about salaries without first obtaining approval?

This problem may seem somewhat insignificant to you, but, as any longtime practicing industrial priest can tell you, the issue is one of honesty and integrity. The very moral fiber of the firm is at stake, particularly if this type of issue is regarded casually. The managing director should adopt the second option above without a second thought. Any priest, finding that his firm accepts the first option, must step forward and challenge the decision maker. The priest must carry it upward as far as necessary to make certain that any decision that is made is based on integrity—and that those involved have learned the relevant lessons.

The salary administrator is also a player in this drama. He was just doing his job but was overruled. He may not have known that the worker had been promised the larger increase. He should be informed that the manager who made the error had been told to follow the guidelines in the future and not to make such promises without approval.

There is an additional related issue that should be examined here. That is, was the original promise reasonable? For example, if the promise had been that the firm would pay for the worker's house, or that the increase would be five hundred percent, we would understand that these promises were not within reason. In such a case, we might more easily accept that the promise could be broken, and that the person who made the promise would be criticized or punished for doing so.

The example, as described, contained a reasonable promise.

Coffee Machine Anthropology?

Here's a much lighter example of what a priest might do, perhaps aided a bit by a clown.

Erik worked as a visiting instructor for a time in a business school in the Netherlands. The organization was of moderate size, some thirty people, including managers, staff, teachers, and course designers. The organization was successful, offering degree courses, courses for industry, and short seminars. Erik could "feel" a positive attitude as he walked through the hallway. He often walked that hallway to the end, where the coffee machine was located.

The coffee was offered free to any staff and students who wanted it. Powdered milk and sugar were offered in small packets that were kept on a shelf on the front of the machine and occasionally were replenished from boxes in a nearby cabinet. Usually, when the supply of sugar and milk was low, the person preparing his or her coffee performed the simple refill task.

One morning, Erik noticed there was no milk or sugar in the shelf on the front of the machine. He refilled both from the boxes and went on his way. Later in the day, he saw that, again, there was no sugar or milk. He began to think about it.

Dutch people are generally polite. They do not take the last cookie on a plate. They do not take the last of the sugar or milk without replenishing it. To Erik, the organization's coffee machine had become an indicator that something was wrong. Somehow, the message being sent by the coffee machine was that attitudes had gone from positive to negative, enough so that some portion of the coffee-drinking staff just did not care.

Erik watched carefully, probably drinking more coffee than usual for the next several days. It was always the same. He found himself replenishing the milk and sugar nearly every time he had coffee. Something was wrong, but what? He had a talk with the man he had come to identify as the priest of the organization. The priest expressed a quite negative view, mostly about the lack of plans for the future. He was concerned that the organization was going nowhere. In fact, the entire staff had had a very unsuccessful meeting a week earlier in which they had attempted to develop a long-range plan but failed.

That was it! Then the clown part of Erik took over. He went to the managing director of the organization and said, "Okay, I know something is wrong, and you're the man who must fix it."

"You have only been here a few days this trip. How do you know?" was the director's reply.

You can imagine the rest of it. After several jokes about the coffee machine and the director himself replenishing the milk and sugar, he went to work on the problem. He had not realized the effect the staff meeting had had. Over several smaller meetings, they began to resolve the issue—and the milk and sugar supplies went back to normal.

The Organization's Values

If an organization has no values, it probably has little need for priests. However, there is no organization without some sort of values, like it or not. This is not to suggest that the priests establish the values; the founders and managers of an organization do that, sometimes with advice from priests. The priests are then useful in helping to keep the values. They are also helpful in seeing that the values are discussed and eventually become second nature to all involved in the work of the organization.

All organizations establish or evolve sets of values by which they operate. Most include such basic values as integrity, respect for the individual, and excellence in their products or services. Consider education—schools and universities: they will often develop a set of values regarding the behavior of their students, integrity in documenting academic research, and political correctness in teaching. Consider police departments: the current wave of accusations regarding racial profiling is causing new values to be adopted. Consider hospitals: most medical institutions have established confidentiality of their patients' medical records as a basic value. The organizational priest is a natural carrier and promoter of these values. Encourage him in this, this extra role he adopts in the workplace.

Do We Have Enough Priests?

How do organizations such as Enron go on and change their cultures, assuming any parts of them do survive? How does an organization that has just completed a merger of two separate corporations establish its new culture? Such questions are not just management problems; they are complex cultural issues and very much the domain of organizational priests. The priests will be the first to analyze the old culture and to identify the elements that need change. As organizational anthropologists, they can chart the steps necessary to begin the change process. As people with a long-term outlook, they can often propose the stages to make this change most efficiently. Firms and other organizations deciding they need culture change would be best advised to include a liberal number of priests on the task forces and committees working on the problem.

In organizations in which the priests are seen as corporate irritants or just ignored, there are probably not enough of them. Human resources departments usually offer a priestly job or two, but the priest role is not normally a full-time job. And it should not become a full-time job, even in an organization that is changing its culture. Yet, part-time priest role players are needed as part of the standard process of meeting organizational goals.

Priests in organizations are not trained for their positions. They are not hired to be priests. They are intuitive people who are good at taking the long view. Generally, they are quiet, not disruptive—unless they find basic principles being violated. A few occasionally become so-called whistle-blowers. Most quietly carry forward what they understand to be the organizational culture. Therefore, you have to make up your own mind as to whether there are enough priests, and if there are not, you have to find them.

Yes, each chapter of this book leaves you with more problems. Find out who your priests are, decide whether you have enough of them, figure out how to find more if you need them, and so on. Remember, it was not a stated objective of this book to solve your problems; its purpose is to give you a new and hopefully better way to think about your organization and its problems.

Priest Role Characteristics

Perhaps a task force charged with making proposals for changing an organization's culture might provide a full-time priest job for a period of time. As with the other roles, the priest job is not usually a full-time one, nor is it the job itself. The priest role is most often performed in the background, quietly, by someone just doing his job—the one he is paid to do. The person playing the priest role can usually be described as some combination of the following:

- future oriented

- intuitive, philosophical

- visionary in outlook

- a good planner

- an historian and anthropologist to the organization

- a carrier of the organization's culture

- a protector of the organization's moral fiber

Naming the Role "Priest"

Some may object to the use of the term "priest" to identify this role, because of its religious connotations. Our industrial priest is not to be confused with the title used in the Roman Catholic religion. We could have just as easily called the role "rabbi" or even "shaman."

The role in modern organizations does have some aspects in common with the roles of religious leaders. The religious leader advises, helps others, and fosters the values of the community. This is the reason we have selected to use the word "priest." Yet there is no intent to relate it to any organized religion. If your organization would prefer another title for the role, please invent one that is more acceptable.

5

The Clown

The role of the clown appears frequently in our literature as well as our anthropological studies. One of the most famous fools, or clowns, as the role is referred to in this book, is found in Shakespeare's *King Lear*. Although the fool seems to be only a half-witted young man, he is the only person close enough to the king, and wise enough and courageous enough, to speak the truth to him. The fool, speaking with innocence and sometimes exaggeration, represents no threat to the king. With his humor, he is able to sometimes say the unthinkable, things that would be unacceptable were he not the fool.

The role of fool, or clown, has been identified in anthropological and psychological studies. In such studies, the fool is sometimes a cult figure, sometimes a trickster, and even at times a person with superhuman qualities. It seems clear from the history of the human race that the fool plays a needed role.

The clown role rounds out our cast of the basic four. The clown, like the priest, is intuitive. He knows the organization and its people. He too, at times, plays the role of corporate anthropologist, examining the functioning of the organization. While the priest is the quiet, thoughtful one, the clown is usually much quicker to act; his humor and sharp wit are nearly always visible. He is the joker, the fool of Shakespeare's plays, the one who chides all the others about their roles and the things they take most seriously. Without the clown, the organization can be less fun and even dreary. Definitely, his role contains the highest risk. He may offend if he goes too far with his quick wit.

The clown role is risky. If he offends often,
he will acquire a "corporate irritant" label.

As indicated earlier, the clown is essential in keeping the hubris and narcissism of the king in check. The clown helps make the power of the king acceptable to the others while making the king appear more human to them. He can do this only if he is quick to understand people, their moods and problems as well as their vanities.

In our modern organizations, the role of clown is the one that involves the most risk. He may function at the very edge of acceptability, occasionally stepping over the edge. One that often steps over the edge may lose his job for that; in the days of Shakespeare, he lost his head for it. Because of this, it may be best for his safety if the clown has a job of some stature in the organization; he may be a manager or a respected, experienced, and valuable worker. He may also function as priest; both roles are certainly intuitive. In other words, it is healthy for the clown to play the role only part time, giving his primary attention to his actual job. Perhaps it is because we have become so serious about our personal business, our organizations, and our pride in our accomplishment that many kings will not tolerate a full-time clown role in their midst.

A Very Simple, Very Light Example

Several years ago, it became evident that a new word had entered a large firm's corporate lexicon. The word was "solutioning." Sometimes such a new word will be used by a top officer of the organization and then be picked up by people working for him; eventually, even his warriors begin to use it, thinking that the king likes the word. ("If it's good enough for him, it's good enough for me.") Speeches were made exhorting the workers to "solution" their problems and become more efficient. High-level managers were saying, "With a little effort, we can 'solution' that."

You can't make up a story like this one; you know it has to be true. People in organizations are adept at altering their speech and behavior to please their superiors, even if they know they sound silly or are behaving inappropriately. The verb "solution" had entered the workers' lives and had begun to corrupt their use of proper English. One of the clowns decided that he must act.

He went to a printing company and had small cards printed; they were about the size of a standard business card. They contained the following: "You used the word *solution* as a verb. This is improper grammar and an example of creeping industrial jargon. Please help me in my crusade to stamp out *solutioning* problems...Let's just *solve* them."

He then faced a more difficult decision. He resolved to stop any meeting in which the offending word was used (politely, of course) and deliver a card to the person who said it. Then came the most difficult decision: what if the meeting was relatively formal, and what if the speaker was a high-level executive? Well, he thought, "I don't have to make that decision until I'm faced with the problem."

He gave away many cards. In fact, he went through the two hundred that made up the minimum printing order in just a few months. Here's how one of the more interesting card deliveries went: The clown and a member of his department, both managers, were reviewing the next year's budget with the controller. Naturally, during the course of the meeting, the offending word was used. In meetings with controllers, there are always problems to solve, or "solution." The clown waited until the controller stopped for a breath and said, "Just a moment, please," and then he handed over a card.

"What the—is this?" the controller asked.

The clown said, "Please just stop and read it." The controller did so and then handed it back. "No," said the clown. "It's now yours; you have earned it." With a bit of muttering, the controller got back to the subject and, a bit later, they concluded the meeting.

One year later, the same two managers were back in the same controller's office reviewing the succeeding year's budget. The clown was pleased to note that the offending word was not used even once. At the end of the meeting, the controller asked, "Did you notice?"

"Notice what?" the clown asked.

"I didn't use that word once," was the controller's reply.

This clown stuff sometimes works quite well. But please be careful

Dave's Piano

This is another story about Dave, the master programmer we met in Chapter 1. Again, Dr. Bob W., who we also met earlier in this book, plays a somewhat risky clown role.

For the better part of a year, as Dave worked on his project, a dialogue had been continuing sporadically in the manager's office next to Dave's workspace. It was a discussion about the need for a new software product: a compiler for what we will call System X. First, the request came to the manager, who, with the help of people in his group, determined that such a product would require some seven person-years, plus associated costs, plus the time of product assurance people and those involved in the company's product-release process. They decided that they did not have that many people who could be released from their tasks to work on it. They therefore requested a "bid" from another division inside the company. Dave was not involved; he was just overhearing these discussions next door.

The bid from the other division was even larger, twelve person-years plus associated costs. They quickly decided that that was too much to spend, based on the forecast for the product. They then sought a bid from another company in the software development business.

Again, the bid was high—ten person-years and all associated costs. Again, after discussing it, they decided not to proceed with the firm or its offer.

By now, our friend Dave was getting bored with the discussion and a bit exasperated with what he thought of as the limited imagination of his neighboring group. He went next door and announced, "If you are serious about wanting this compiler for System X, I'll be happy to do it in one year; I'll need one person to assist." In other words, it was a bid of two person-years.

The manager was astonished. "Two people for one year? I don't believe it." But he did ask if Dave thought he could be freed from his present work to begin immediately. Dave thought that might be possible, but they would have to consult with his manager.

The manager agreed and Dave and an assistant went to work on the project. As promised, in one year, they had finished and it was ready for the product quality people to test it. In fact, no one had believed it would be ready on time, so there was no schedule for a review by the quality department, and therefore more than the usual scramble occurred before the new product could be released.

Dr. Bob W. heard the story of the project from Dave himself, about eighteen months after his compiler had been released as a product. Bob asked Dave questions about the work: how big the project was, why the others had bid so high, and so on. It turned out to be about seventy thousand lines of software code, a complex undertaking for that time, but, as Dave pointed out, it was not the first compiler he had written. Then Bob asked about quality, its performance after being released. As of that point, after eighteen months of use, it had sustained two "bugs," or errors, one in Dave's product and the other in the operating system, not a part of Dave's product.

If you are associated with the software business in any way, you will know that the amount of work Dave did in that short a period, plus the lack of bugs in the final product, represents an amazing accomplishment. Bob asked Dave whether he had been rewarded in any special way. He said, "Well, not yet; I've heard that over in the managing director's office they're discussing that." Bob asked how much he thought he would receive as a reward or what promotion he would receive. "No promotion," he said. "They are discussing a reward of $5,000."

"What!" Bob exclaimed, "we saved at least five person-years, the product was released on schedule, the quality is extremely high, and they are talking about only $5,000. That's ridiculous!"

"Don't bother about it," replied Dave. "I bought my own reward." Of course, Bob asked about it. Dave said that he had always wanted a grand piano and decided that this was the time to buy one for himself. In those days, the early 1980s, a grand piano cost about $3,000 per foot, measured from the keyboard to the far end of the instrument. Dave had bought a seven-footer, as large as the space in his home would accommodate. He invited Bob over for a concert. He accepted.

Bob thought about Dave, his accomplishment, and his "reward" for a few days, and then he called the managing director. Of course, Bob found himself speaking to an assistant. The assistant verified that they had sought the advice of a very experienced software development manager and that they were settling on a reward of $5,000 for Dave. Bob exploded into strong words about what they had saved, the quality of the product, the on-time delivery, and so on, ending with, "Please tell the director I think he is a cheap son of a bitch."

"Sorry," said the assistant, "my life is too short to say things like that to my boss. If you want him to know what you think of him, you'll have to tell him yourself."

"Okay," Bob said, "will you please organize the meeting?"

The meeting took place at the end of a long day of work in a nicely furnished corner office. The participants were the managing director; his assistant, who had a slight smile on his face; the "expert," who had recommended the amount of the reward; and Dr. Bob, the clown of this little drama. He spoke first.

"Thank you for agreeing to hold this meeting." He reviewed the purpose, Dave's accomplishment, and the money and time that had been saved, and then he ended by saying to the director, "I'm told you think that was worth only $5,000. I'm here to tell you that you are nothing but a cheap son of a bitch."

"Maybe so. We'll see," said the director. He then asked the "expert" to review his data on other reward amounts. He began with a very logical and orderly presentation, which Bob interrupted after about a minute. He said, "You're being so logical. I am not here for a rational discussion. Don't you guys understand? This is an emotional subject. If you guys really understood your business—and your worker—you would know precisely how large this award should be."

"How much?" asked the director. Bob replied that it should be $21,000. "What!" exclaimed the director. "Not $20,000 or $25,000? How did you come up with an odd number like $21,000?"

Bob explained that if they really knew their man, Dave, they would know that he got tired of waiting and bought his own reward for his accomplishment. Bob told them that Dave had purchased a grand piano, that pianos of that type went for $3,000 per foot, and that he had bought a seven-foot piano. The meeting was terminated shortly after that.

Of course, the award was not raised to $21,000. These things do not happen that way. But the amount was raised to $10,000.

Did you see the various roles that took shape in this little drama? They are relatively easy to identify: a king (the director), two warriors (the assistant and the expert), and the clown (Bob). Of course, Dave played the master warrior. Don't be mistaken about the lack of a priest, someone who wanted to make sure that justice was achieved. The managing director was certainly part priest, and Bob knew that he also had a bit of the priest within himself. The meeting would not have been possible without some priestly thinking. It also would not have been possible if the king had had no tolerance for clowns. Notice that the clown role in this example was somewhat risky—Bob had to play with a bit of panache to achieve any success at all. Note also that there was no personal gain for Bob as any part of the outcome. An altruistic intent is another characteristic of the clown role, properly played.

Identifying Your Organization's Clowns

The clowns in any of today's organizations may be somewhat difficult to find. First, there aren't many of them. With the egos and hubris of the authority figures, the kings, being what they are, many will make it quite clear that they have no need, and indeed little tolerance, for any clowns at all in their organizations. In spite of all the nice words about King Lear's jester and the hubris of kings requiring the balancing influence of the fool, or clown, we do not see this role played very often. The lack of clowns represents an imbalance in many of our modern organizations.

In the makeup and dress of the circus, clowns are easy to identify. They are colorful, have perpetual smiles (or frowns) painted on their faces, and are expected to entertain us. Probably the most famous of these clowns was Emmett Kelly, a circus clown of some years ago. Another was Bozo. Without the disguise to protect the identity of the clown, the role is one of high risk and seemingly little return to the role player. Where would you find such people in modern organizations? Perhaps the clown uniform still exists and we just need to know how to spot it. There are a few modern-day organizational clowns who are older, perhaps nearing retirement, who have announced their role by their appearance. I knew just such a man a few years ago. He was balding, and he had let his remaining hair grow into clumps at the sides of his head; he took to wearing bright yellow suspenders, no matter whether they matched his suits. (And he did wear business suits—after all, he held an important job in a New York bank.) His sense of humor and sharp wit made him an essential part of many meetings. His clown performances were in high demand, not only for their humor but also for the real value he added to the firm's management meetings.

I met another such clown role player a few years ago in a human resources department. Again, he was older, nearing retirement. He once said, "The company would have to pay me more if they fired me than if they let me continue to work." He would sit in staff meetings and help the human resources process work, as they discussed serious issues relating to salaries, promotions, terminations, and executive resources. He was fearless in these meetings; he would challenge anyone, from worker to king, if he thought it would help.

Therefore, perhaps one characteristic of some of our modern-day clowns is the freedom to play the role—that is, the protection of an assured retirement income if something goes wrong. These two men were not risking a chance for promotion—they had already reached their highest level, or at least they thought so. That too, gave them greater freedom to act as they saw fit. Clowns are usually quite comfortable at being who they are. They are not usually vying for a top king position or other forms of gain.

Another way to identify a person who may be a clown is to observe carefully the process that takes place in meetings. A clown is expert at communication between people. If you find a person who, meeting after meeting, seems to be able to sit quietly until just the right moment and then enter a comment or recommendation that completely changes the tone and helps the meeting to produce a better result, you have probably found a clown. The clown, in a meeting, will usually play a quiet, even self-effacing, role through most of it. When he does make his intervention, he will do it with humor and always with a well-thought-out suggestion. However, do not be misled: a clown presents his own point of view on the issues being discussed—he is not in the meeting merely because he enjoys the process.

In fact, the clown is probably the best of the four roles at the communication process. Clowns understand the people involved in a human process better than the others. Modern organizational anthropologists, called in to consult with a firm or other type of organization, would be well advised to seek out a few of the organization's clowns first and listen carefully to what these people have to say about their organizations. Need we remind consultants to protect information given in confidence? The clown role is already risky enough without a consultant increasing the danger.

Those playing the clown role are usually not "bucking for promotion." They may not be among the organization's managers, although that role combination is certainly possible. If not nearing retirement, they will at least have the security that frees them to do what they think is best.

They may have protection. That is, a clown may have a kind of senior "protector," a person, often at a higher level, perhaps somewhere distant in the organization, who acts as advisor to the clown and who will, on request, step in to defend the action of the clown. Sometimes such a defender will be the king; more often, it will be a senior person near the king in the organization.

However he has developed the security to play the clown role, the clown is not playing it for himself. He views it as a kind of conflict of interest to use his human process skills to advance himself or line his own pockets. He is playing for the organization. He is committed to the values and goals of the organization, and those are the driving forces behind his actions. One of the most rewarding moments for a clown is to see the "elephant" change course by a degree or two as a result of his actions. Organizations are often like large animals, set in their ways and often quite difficult to steer.

As we saw earlier, this commitment to the values and goals of the organization is also the motivation of the priest. It is not exactly altruism that these two role players are exhibiting. It is something more than that. They are also motivated to meet their regular goals as warriors or kings; they view these general clown or priest role objectives as additional. Clowns and priests, in playing their roles provide some of the glue that holds the organization together.

Staff Work

Clowns enjoy staff positions more than line positions. They prefer to have jobs that are in the more complex parts of the organizational web. They like jobs entitled "assistant to…" They are comfortable in jobs in headquarters. Their friends, the true warriors and kings, think this preference is crazy. "Why would you take a job in that mess?" they will ask their clown friends.

Yet the clown sees such jobs quite differently. His view is that work in the direct line of command is finite, defined by specific goals and objectives. He knows that once he has learned to do the job it will eventually become boring to him because of its finiteness. He sees staff work as infinite, with possibilities for much more than full-time work. Staff work, to him, is a job in which the values and goals of the organization most closely match the goals of his job. Our clown friend, Dr. Bob, once went from a job managing a 150-person software development center to a job in the division's human resources department. This was the job mentioned earlier, with the position description, "Evaluate the motivational environment in…[the division] and propose change." There was never a job closer to Bob's clown perspective. His friends thought he had taken leave of his senses. "What happened to you? Did you get demoted for some failure?" they wanted to know. Bob simply pointed out that he had gotten a salary increase and thought the job would be very interesting. It looked like a promotion to him.

There may be a clue here for any kings who wish to know where their clowns can be most effective. Staff work is probably a good answer. Human resources, some accounting jobs, education and training, and other positions that are attached to the organization and help keep it running are all good candidates. However, staff jobs should not become life sentences for your clowns. They need change just as much as everyone else does. They need line jobs, in a way, as training for their future staff jobs. In the same way, warriors should have occasional staff jobs as training for future king roles so they can gain a better perspective, from the inside, of how the organization works. This is true of large, complex organizations; in small organizations, those with one hundred people or less, a clown can be effective nearly anywhere. He can see and understand the workings of the entire organization from any vantage point.

Clown Role Characteristics

Note again that the role is not the job; the role player plays it when he thinks it is needed. The clown role is rarely, if ever, full time. If it is, it is most likely a temporary job on a committee or task force to help construct a long-range plan or to plan the merger of two large organizations. Our clowns are somewhat scarce; this may be a result of the risk associated with the role. In spite of the risk, we do have clowns in our organizations. People playing the clown role can usually be described as some combination of the following:

• people oriented

• intuitive

• willing to take risks

- an excellent communicator

- a good facilitator

- likely to prefer the complexity of staff work over line work

- a catalyst in meetings

- not playing the role for personal gain

> *Clowns make work more fun—and more productive.*

6

It's the Culture

The four roles have existed in one form or another since the early days of the human race. As soon as there were hunters and gatherers, and later, Stone Age builders, humans learned that they achieved better results if they worked in groups. They could defend themselves more successfully if they joined forces with each other. Hence, the first organizations contained warriors, some sort of leader, a shaman or priest, and a fool or clown. In the preceding four chapters, the roles are described as they are now observed in our modern organizational world.

So far in this book, the word *culture* has appeared several times. It was used to refer to the practices and values of modern industrial organizations. The priest and the clown were both portrayed as carriers of an organization's culture. It is beliefs, practices, and values that make up a culture, and it is this definition that we will use as we continue to consider the roles we play in our organizational life.

Every organization has a language of its own, reflecting its culture.

Our democratic, capitalistic ideas and practices influence our modern organizations; these ideas and practices provide a sort of umbrella under which modern business organizations operate. The business culture we are considering was formed for the most part during the twentieth century. Let's now briefly consider the elements that make up the setting for our modern organizations.

We will not provide an analysis of our Western culture and its development. Many highly qualified writers have done that. An excellent book to read if you want examine our Western culture is *From Dawn to Decadence*, by Jacques Barzun (2000). Here, we will simply list a few of the general influences our larger culture, and our still evolving business culture, has on our workplaces and our workers.

1. Democratic Institutions

We live in a democracy. We believe people have a right to be heard and to partic-
ipate in selecting their government officials. We in America live in a free society
whose goal is to preserve "life, liberty, and the pursuit of happiness." We do our
best to influence our society and its ways of operating—in business, in education,
in medical care, and in all other areas of society. We practice free trade, but with
limitations, on agricultural products and textiles, to cite two examples.

In business, we operate at somewhat less than full liberal democracy. We usually find CEOs or presidents at the top, who may be selected by boards of directors. These top officers can perform their functions by acting as dictators,
benevolent dictators, or aristocrats, or they can be people who act as little like
monarchs as possible. The latter try to operate in such a way that they provide
their workers with as much individual empowerment as possible. The dictators
among the top corporate officers are usually the most intolerant of priests and
clowns. A few companies have management committees at the top, but these usually include a top officer who is there when someone asks, "Who's the boss here?"

While our businesses operate under a democratic government and follow generally democratic principles, most operate with a top-down command structure.
There are rules, rulebooks, controls, and, in most firms, a bureaucratic system
that limits individual freedom to make decisions. They are power-based structures, just as are democratic governments. It is the power base that can lead to
ego, narcissism, and other diseases of power-hungry managers who actually
repress their workers, particularly if there are no priests and clowns present.

2. Military Structures

The structure of our organizations, particularly business organizations, has been
heavily influenced by military structures, particularly those that evolved during
World War II. There is always a person at the top, the commanding general, the
CEO, or, as he is referred to in this book, the player of the king role. There are
line and *staff* functions in our organizations, names that came directly from the
military. Line functions are found on the organization charts by following lines of
command, through levels headed by lesser generals, and downward to the warrior
level. Staffs are usually attached to various levels but do not have the multilevel
structure of the line functions.

The concepts of *command* and *control* are key elements in the ways of thinking
and doing in both military and business. If the top officer sees his job mainly as

one of command and control, he may not tolerate priests and clowns; he may not see the need for them.

As with the military, our business managers believe in clear definitions of responsibilities and authority. They provide limited freedom to fail. "After all, we're in business to make a profit." Their attitudes toward failure are "The buck stops here" and "It can't happen on my watch."

The command orientation of our business managers represents another entry to power and therefore runaway egos. The more power is unrestrained, the more likely the system will be to limit and even repress its workers. Repression? Here in the freedom-loving West? Consider the worker holding on to his job to support his family at even twice the minimum wage, and with limited or no health benefits. Dictatorial decisions by power-hungry managers can be more repressive than they were under Communism. Restraining greed and the desire for more and more power is the job of those playing the roles of priests and clowns.

As commitment to the military approach increases, the tolerance for priests and clowns decreases. If you are a clown and your manager has a small cannon ornamenting his desk, and if his stories are often about General George Patton, beware: your life as a clown in that organization may be a short one.

3. Capitalism

We operate a capitalistic business system. That is, it is based on money, making a profit, salesmanship, markets, market niches, ownership, and the stock market—in short, it is based on money as its primary measurement. Interestingly, studies have shown that workers under the old Soviet system felt a stronger sense of identity with their work and their work organizations than do most workers in our modern capitalistic system.

Once again, using money as the basic measure leads to greed for more, and thus for more power. It leads to excessive attention to quarterly results and to the need to falsify records if the results are not satisfactory. Recent news stories of companies cheating their owners and employees make clear the need for stronger accounting overview—and the need for more priests and clowns to be active within our business firms, publicly acting as whistle-blowers, if necessary.

4. Male Ego Driven

Dictatorial top managers and managers who are militarily command and control oriented are often male and male ego driven. The disease of kings, hubris, mentioned earlier, is the most common example of an overactive male ego. The driving force for some of our kings to become dictatorial as they take on their kingship roles is clearly a male ego characteristic. There is as yet less experience with females in dictatorial king roles, but we may safely assume that they too are not immune from this ego problem.

Some "maleness" in roles and organizations is deemed necessary if we are to make a profit, meet our objectives, and manage our financial resources. However, if this kind of maleness—if that's really what it is—is not sufficiently balanced by the leavening agents of intuition, values, and ideas, then we are operating with excessive maleness. This may be a weakness that women's equal entry into our business organizations may help to repair. Priests and clowns were the balancing factors in several of our organizational stories. If women represent a way to provide more strength in the priest and clown roles, let's get on with the rebalancing needed, and let's ask not only women but all those who can help to provide better balance, whether male or female, to assist. Of course, women make good warriors and kings as well. We should encourage them in those roles too.

5. Careers: Higher Is Better?

My two grandmothers, who provided most of my inspiration as I was growing up, made it very clear that they wanted me to "go places." They imparted the wisdom that "higher is better." Although they were never able to be much more specific, the message they left with me was that wherever I went to work, I should stay for as many years as I could, rise to the highest level possible, and get the gold watch at retirement.

With that as the goal, our modern industrial organizations made it clear that I would have to begin as a warrior and do my best. The best warriors, these organizations made clear, were candidates for *management*. If that's the reward for the best warrior, take it with no questions asked. So I did, only four years after beginning my working life as a warrior. I never could believe that I could become the typical king. Instead, I became so thoughtful about the change that had happened that I was asked to describe it in one of the management schools offered by the company. I took that as a positive indicator that I was succeeding, but I was never quite certain that I was becoming good at the king role. In fact, I found myself on tranquilizers shortly afterward, prescribed for stress. The real kings above me in the structure expressed concern about that, and I suspected that they watched me more closely to see if "I would ever measure up." Real kings, it seemed, did not have to go on tranquilizers.

Our industrial world today is fixed on the idea that the best warriors are candidates for higher levels of employment—candidates for kingship. Some, those with a good sense of working with people and the ability to manage while empowering their workers to take responsibility, make very good kings. Some warriors do not turn out this way. Some are just not good management candidates; some are much better candidates for senior, master-level warrior jobs—even if their pay scales fall short of what is possible in management.

Whatever happened to the idea that to become a manager, or king, one should have the qualifications, aptitude, and personal characteristics for that new profession? It really is a change in professions from that of many of our warriors. Going from salesman to manager is a change in profession. So is going from engineer or scientist to manager. So is going from teacher to school principal. This rather casual transition process is one of the weaknesses in the system as it exists today. Overall it produces less than the best managers, while at the same time removing some of the best warriors from their warrior roles.

6. The Salary Gap

Along with the notion that the best warriors should advance to kingship, there is an increasing difference in pay between the warrior and the king. Several years ago, a study in Japan concluded that the highest-level manager should average some seven times the average worker, or warrior, level of pay. Today, particularly in the United States, the reality is far from that. Top managers are paid literally hundreds of times what their working warriors are paid. This includes salary, bonuses, stock options, and other benefits. In the United States today, the average chief executive "pay" is some five hundred times that of the average worker. In most European countries, that ratio is only some ten to twenty times. The following is from the *New York Times*, "Market Watch" section, January 25, 2004:

Table 1.1
Chief Executive Pay as a Multiple of Employee Average

Country	Multiple of Employee Average
United States	531
Brazil	57
Mexico	45
Britain	25
Canada	21
France	16
Germany	11
Japan	10

We live in a culture that seems to hold salary, or income, as one of the most important measures of success. Perhaps the real issue here, particularly at the high end of the scale, is greed. Whether or not that is true, the message conveyed to the working warrior, looking up, is that he is a fool to settle for remaining as a "common worker," particularly if he is offered the opportunity to become a king. He believes this even if he is not particularly interested in that kind of work and even if he likes his warrior work so much that he would prefer to stay with it for a lifetime of work and achieve mastery at that work.

At its most extreme, the greed resulting from the focus on what it is possible to "earn" results in the scandals we have seen of late: Enron and other examples of corporate dishonesty designed to "improve the financial results" beyond reality. The gap between what is possible for a good warrior to earn and what many executive level kings are being paid is one of the more serious problems with the present system. It requires attention and repair immediately. As long as the gap is as large as it is, we cannot blame our good warriors if they are drawn into the greed system. They, too, may have had grandmothers who wanted them to achieve the highest possible level.

7. Protection for Failing Firms

In spite of our commitment to capitalism and free trade, there is a trend in the United States (which has also begun to show up in Europe) to protect failing companies and even entire industries from having to go out of business—that is, from failing. Government subsidies for companies that cannot be sufficiently competitive protect them from having to admit that their management has failed. This trend causes warriors to lose jobs while many of the kings continue to draw their unreasonably high salaries and bonuses. That is not fair. What this practice communicates to the warrior is, "Take the management job; even if you fail, it doesn't matter."

This is another soft spot in our organizational culture.

Power, Greed, and Egos

The list of our business organizations' characteristics presented here admittedly may focus too much attention on power, greed, and the business ego. But is it inaccurate? Of course, there are exceptions. In the first five chapters of this book, all the stories of priests and clowns providing balance and surviving in their jobs are examples of managers willing to do what is right and debate principles. Yet, a quick review of our daily business news will usually produce examples that attest to the above list and that the business culture lacks balance.

This is the message of this book: The four roles are needed in balance in our business organizations—not necessarily in equal numbers but in sufficient numbers of each. All four roles are needed for successful working groups, and working groups or teams are definitely necessary in our complex organizations of today. The present American business organizational culture is becoming increasingly unbalanced. Left alone, our clowns and priests will disappear; our kings will become more hubristic, greedy, and dictatorial. The situation cannot be fixed by government or corporate decree or by increasing numbers of lawyers. We must all take the initiative to fix it.

Changes in the Culture

There are several significant movements and experiments that are influencing the existing organizational culture. These are attempts to change the culture, improve it, or shed light on new ways of managing that might make organizations more effective.

One of the most obvious is the women's movement, with its long-term emphasis on equal opportunity, fair promotion practices, and equal pay for equal work. In the long term, this will allow us to use an entire half of our working population more effectively. It will also make inroads into the archaic male-driven organization and management styles we still encounter in most industries and government branches.

Another change is the overt attempt to diminish the ego and hubris of kings. It is simply a series of trial and error experiments to reduce the ego trappings of kingly status. For example, there is a large firm in the textile industry that permits no manager at any level to have a private office. Their kings operate in cubicles, just like the warriors on staff, in accounting, in computer support, and everywhere else. Of course, there are still workers that have no cubicles; they work on assembly lines, but they have equal access, when needed, to the various meeting rooms when discussions are to take place about the business.

Experiments abound these days in different approaches to organizational structure. These include various types of teams, some with no managers at all, most with team leaders, some of which rotate the management task over time through the entire team. One of the more unusual experiments is taking place in a Brazilian company called Semco. Here, employees make decisions regarding the company's finances, its products, and even how much they are paid. In fact, Semco is no longer an experiment; it is an operating reality. Ricardo Semler, its CEO, describes it in a book *Maverick: The Success Story Behind the World's Most Unusual Workplace* (1993). Do not be misled; the term CEO here means something different from the usual. The entire operation is much closer to a liberal democracy than that of most companies. And it works! In its first decade, the company grew rapidly, in spite of the wild swings in the Brazilian economy during the same period.

These are just a few examples. The number and extent of the experiments taking place indicates that we are trying to improve our ways of organizing and doing business. The successes will, of course, make their way to other companies via consultants. The failures will be forgotten, but with luck, the lessons learned will be documented. These many and various attempts bode well for the future of our organizational cultures and our capitalistic system. In other words, we are definitely not locked into a system that we cannot change. We are growing and improving it as we go along.

Change Needed

This brief review of our organizational culture indicates that our businesses and other types of organizations are still quite military and male oriented, many excessively so. Yes, they are democratic, for the most part. However, many organizations suffer from unfettered male egos, demonstrated by the salary gap, greed, and corporate scandals mentioned above. In spite of the experiments and trends now taking place, we are still not learning enough of the lessons.

A quick examination of any large firm in the United States today would quickly reveal king and warrior roles at work. These two roles are easy to identify everywhere. On the other hand, one might have to search for evidence of many playing the roles of priest and clown. In fact, these two roles are so scarce that one making such a study might have to remind himself periodically of the definitions of these two roles in order to make certain they haven't seen and failed to recognize them.

Most of our work is described in terms of management and worker tasks. Players of king and warrior roles do most of our work. Is all of the work contained in these two roles? A look at management training courses and business school offerings would suggest that it is. Human resources staffs may offer some priestly services to their companies, but even in this department there are pressures to be expedient, regardless of values and standards of fair play.

We are dominated by the king and warrior roles. We have to search for the priest and clown roles. If successful organizations require all four roles, we are clearly living in a time of imbalance. More priests and more clowns, please!

7

More Clowns and Priests

Do you see many clowns and priests quietly doing their jobs in the firm in which you work? Do you easily find them in our public school systems? If the answer to these questions is that you do not see many clowns and priests in your day-to-day work and family environment, you now know one of the reasons that some fool decided to write this book. There are not enough people playing these roles. In fact, there is much evidence that we are suffering from a shortage of clowns and priests. Left alone, clowns and priests will disappear, and kings will become more susceptible to their kingly diseases of hubris, ego, and greed.

Martin Luther King's work is perhaps one of the best examples of someone playing the role of the priest to sponsor change in our society.

And in our business firms? Most visible are the accounting scandals and the executives being fired (but with huge separation payments and stock options). Corporate executives and consultants write books about success (measured in money and power) and leadership, spelled out in terms of king and warrior roles. Not much is being said about creating and protecting priest and clown roles anywhere in our business culture.

These days, we have resorted to attack by lawsuits to solve problems that could have been resolved by a clown or priest. The growth of litigation and lawyers is one of the results of the clown and priest shortage. With the egos of our industrial kings allowed to run free, we have governmental regulation, unfair competition suits, and unrealistically high compensation for executives. Tightening the reins on our kings is difficult, if not impossible, without the aid of clowns and priests.

Whistle-Blowers

Remember the Enron whistle-blower, Sherron Watkins? She was an executive with the firm who tried to warn Enron Chairman Ken Lay that the firm was engaged in questionable accounting practices. Her now-famous memo to Lay, dated August 15, 2001, said, in part, "I am incredibly nervous that we will implode in a wave of accounting scandals." A reading of the various press reports on the role that she played in the Enron scandals suggests that she was playing the role of priest, or possibly the clown. Yes, she was vice president of corporate development at Enron; does this make her sole role that of king? Not necessarily. She was probably playing a role that was mostly priest, advising the firm on fundamental principles that she believed were being broken. Whistle-blowers are often those playing clown or priest roles and who become frustrated and decide to formally document their concerns (and, in some cases, to make them public). It is doubtful that Sherron Watkins went public voluntarily. Her public appearance was brought about after her memo was discovered during the investigation of Enron's finances.

Adhering to the basic values of the organization and the society in which it operates is the issue here. In other words, it is adhering to the values of the culture: the society's culture, the organization's culture, and even the department's culture. The basics are visible; our schools and our religions establish them. Integrity, honesty, and respectful treatment of others are some of the basics. Then, in addition, some firms establish values relative to customer service, product quality, responsible corporate citizenship within the community, and the respectful treatment of their employees and clients, for example. These values are the domain of the clowns and priests as they help their organizations follow them. Whether or not the values are established formally makes little difference. With the help of the priests in organizations, everyone knows the basic values. The clowns are there when needed to call attention, in an acceptable way, to those not adhering to the values.

Imbalance?

So there are some priests and clowns. Unfortunately, there is no registry of priests and clowns, so data cannot be presented here showing a gradual decline in these two roles. Observation is all we have to go on, so you will have to judge for yourself.

One measure was referred to in the last chapter. That is the increasing gap between executive pay and worker pay, especially in the United States. This increase may be in part due to insufficient numbers of clowns and priests advising their kings.

Another indication is the variety of "patches" being put on various organizations by those who have recognized some imbalance and tried to patch up the system. One such patch is the establishment of mentors in many organizations.

Mentors are advisors to workers; as such, they are playing a priest role. They assist in career planning, but they are for the most part a company benefit, such as training, that workers can use as they feel they need the service.

Another such experiment, in vogue several years ago, was the creation of the "ombudsman", a person to whom one could go to air complaints and grievances and who could advise management of problems without having to involve the person who made the complaint. Again, the program acted as a patch on the system, a sort of safety valve; it was not an integral part of the system but was something tacked on. Similarly, most labor unions offer processes for airing grievances. While these grievance processes are part of the system, they are too often seen by some in management as just another form of irritation.

Mentors, ombudsmen, and grievance processes helped organizations in which executives knew there were problems. All of these were patches to improve the environment of the worker and his need to tell someone in power that things were not working properly. However, none of these programs replaced the growing need to improve the balance between the king-warrior roles and the priest-clown roles. None addressed the diseases of kings—narcissism, hubris, and greed.

We have a choice: we can address the imbalance by adding more rules, procedures, and laws to our already highly bureaucratic management systems, or we can learn how to achieve better balance.

Achieving Better Balance

How can we achieve better balance in our organizations? Is some sort of legal action or new regulation required? Definitely not. More laws and more regulation are the opposite of what we need. Individual workers, as well as some of the more philosophically oriented kings, can help to right the imbalance. A grassroots, inside-the-organization "positive conspiracy" is what is needed. Here are a few ideas that may help you to evaluate your organization and begin the process of improving its balance.

The first step is to identify some of your organization's priests and clowns and encourage them to embrace these roles. Anyone can do this, whether you occupy a king or warrior role. Most organizations have people who are playing a priest or clown, or both roles, sometimes quite visibly and sometimes very much in the background. You may want to go back and take a second look at Chapters 4 and 5 to improve your ability to identify these people and to learn some of the questions to ask them about what they are doing.

Suppose you can't find any people playing priest or clown roles in your organization. If the organization has existed for five years or more, and if it has twenty-five or more people, please search a second time. At minimum, your organization has a few people who at least have the characteristics of these role players. If not, have a talk with a manager or some other responsible person; show him this book, recommend that he read it, and then begin a discussion about the general subject of these two roles and whether they are needed. Chances are this will start some thinking about the organization and its long-range future.

Assuming you have found some people playing priest and clown roles, set out to learn from them about the history and culture of your organization. Learn about its basic principles. Listen to some of their "war stories" about the good times and the more stressful times. Ask for examples in which the rules were broken and ask about values that have persisted from the beginning of the organization. Enjoy this work and learn from it, for it is a fun task. Your priests and clowns love to talk about these things; this love is part of their ability to foster the corporate culture.

Once you have begun these discussions, think about how you might help the priests and clowns as they spread the culture and principles. Maybe you will find one of these roles worth considering for yourself in the long term. On that thought, consider another aspect of the balance question. What and where are the jobs in your organization that are most likely to be occupied by those playing the role of priest or clown? Human resources staffs represent good possibilities. One of the most potentially powerful positions for a person who plays a part-time priest or clown role is secretary or assistant to the boss. Company education and training departments often have priests or clowns. Teaching, after all, can be an opportunity for strengthening the corporate culture and its values. Jobs involving planning for the future of the organization represent additional possibilities. Perhaps some of these represent future opportunities for you. At minimum, they offer you a chance to further evaluate your organization by deciding for yourself whether people who want to play priest or clown roles fill some of these jobs.

If you are able to do so, encourage the creation of at least a few jobs that offer greater participation by priests and clowns. As we have just said, these jobs probably already exist in human resources. They also may be found on corporate and divisional staffs. If you think such a job might be good for you at some point in your future work life, try to land one for yourself. Remember that priest and clown roles are not played for personal gain; they are for the gain of the organization—and they should be fun.

If You Are a King...

You have some additional work to do as you learn from your priests and clowns. Offer support to those playing these roles. Find out when and where they have been frustrated when trying to keep the corporate culture glued together. Offer to help them by supplying additional information about the organization's values and goals. Find ways to involve them more in planning processes, and draw out their ideas for the organization's future.

Another way to help if you are one of the organization's king role players is to find out whether some protection is needed for your priests and clowns as they play these roles. It may be that you can become a better protector and supporter as these people need one. All they usually need is someone with whom they can discuss problems they have identified. It's better for them to have such discussions with you, or with others responsible for issues they are addressing, than to try to solve problems outside the normal way of doing things in your organization.

The role that is in shortest supply is that of clown. Encourage your clowns if you can find them. Encourage people who can play this role to join your organization. Help protect your organization's clowns and encourage them in their mission to defuse the narcissism and hubris of the ego-driven kings. Notice the repeated use of the word *encourage*—we do not need training courses for clowns; all we need to do is encourage them in what they are already doing. If you are a king, listen more carefully to your clowns and try to change your behavior if you have seriously thought about a clown's message and realize that he has made a valid point.

If you are a king, think very carefully before you criticize, demote, or fire a clown for playing that role. Yes, you are within your rights as king to conclude that, as far as you are concerned, he is a corporate irritant. However, before you go too far, have a look at yourself and your performance. Ask a trusted colleague whether you exhibit too much ego. If the reply is affirmative, seek professional help. Then, don't fire the clown; give him a raise.

Philosopher Kings

How is an organization's king to function if he must hear out his priests and clowns and still meet his goals for revenues, profits, and growth? The king must become more philosophical as the organization grows. He must change as his organization changes. We referred to this in Chapter 3; now we will address the changes he must make more explicitly.

At the beginning, when a small organization is just established, the manager, owner, or boss is mostly warrior and part-time leader of his team or small family-like group. As the organization grows to twenty-five people or more, the boss, or king role player, must become a true manager—not a military commander, but a manager. This means he must develop some of the philosopher's thoughtfulness, which can be fostered by a priest inside the organization. The first step is to identify the priest. He is there—he has been there since the beginning—so the art of the manager now is to identify the priest and listen to what he has to say.

By the time the organization reaches two hundred, the king must have evolved further. Now he is a manager over managers, in short, an executive who must get things done through the cooperation of others. To do that he has a choice: either develop their trust and respect or make rules and command them to follow. The first requires the assistance of some priests and clowns; the second leads to bureaucracy and the diseases of kings.

In other words, the king himself must change as the organization grows. This is particularly true if the organization's original family-style warmth is to be retained through many years of growth. Failure to change, the king will learn, will cause the organization to falter at some level, usually somewhere in the range of fifty to one hundred people. It will level off in revenues and growth generally until the king grows to the next required stage—or until he is asked to resign and does so.

As an organization grows, its king must undergo a process of transformation. He begins as a warrior, much as all the others. Then he becomes a leader of his group of warriors, but he is still one of them much of his time. He then must become more of a manager, and in doing so give up some of his warrior tasks. In his manager role, he spends much of his time on financial concerns—budgets, profits, and taxes. He also spends time hiring, determining salaries, and acquiring more office space—he is becoming an administrator. Eventually he must become an executive, representing his organization to the rest of the world, in short, a statesman. Failure to transform himself means failure to the entire organization.

What is needed therefore are "philosopher kings." These are kings who think through what they must become as their organizations change around them. These are kings who adapt, who change themselves, with the assistance of their priests and clowns, as well as their warriors, as they and their family-style organizations grow and prosper. Those kings who fail to grow in this fashion become despots, rulers who dominate through bureaucratic rules, personal power, and personal aggrandizement.

An Afterthought: Playing More than One Role

These four roles are not lifetime sentences for each of us, although it may seem that they have been described as such. Most of us are complex mixtures of interests, capabilities, and behavioral patterns. Some, as indicated earlier, become intoxicated with their role and let it dominate them. Others may exhibit elements of all four roles. We are all free to change as we go along; however, intuitive people will generally remain mostly intuitive and the rational/operational will generally remain rational/operational.

Role combinations are not only possible but also common. Philosopher kings have been known throughout history. These are people who play their kingly roles with more intuition than most, and usually this combination produces a king less likely to suffer from hubris.

Since most clowns and priests must work to earn their living, they usually are working as warriors, thus producing more role combinations. Clown-priests can be found, practicing both the insightful planning of the priest and the use of humor to call attention to problems when necessary. Most of us combine whatever skills we have and play whatever roles we can to assist our organizations to be the best at what they do and, at the same time, to follow sound principles.

A word of caution is in order here. It is all too easy to refer to people, as we did earlier with "King George," using the role names as labels. We may too quickly say, "He's nothing but a clown" or "He acts like he's our priest. What's the matter with him?" Using role names as labels can be harmful to both people and the organization. Therefore, think before you use these role names to refer to individuals.

8

Talk about It

Where do we go from here? Is this a call for a noisy revolution in our industrial and other organizations? Definitely not. A quietly managed, positive conspiracy is what these organizations require. In some ways, a noisy revolution may be easier to start and to manage. It is often more difficult to begin and manage slow and gradual change. Nevertheless, the gradual approach is recommended here. We in our developed Western world have created organizations that work, and often work very well. Still, they can be improved, some of them much improved.

To summarize the problem: our workplaces are becoming increasingly bureaucratic and less fun for workers. Increasingly narcissistic and greedy managers who exercise their male egos in top-down direction setting, too often called "leadership" by management consultants drive our growing bureaucracy. The rules, legal actions, and bureaucracy are overwhelming existing natural forces that normally keep our organizations in balance. These natural forces can be found from the days of the earliest human organizations up to the present. These forces are provided by those playing the fundamental roles, not just the kings and warriors but the priests and clowns who attempt to provide balance. These two balancing roles can be found today in many organizations, but in insufficient numbers and with insufficient influence.

First, a Foolish Suggestion

We suggest making it illegal for kings to "earn" more than one hundred times their average worker's earnings. Unfortunately, this would just make more work for lawyers and would be highly profitable to offshore banks and financial institutions willing to maintain their clients' privacy. You see, it's clearly a foolish suggestion. How about this, then: all kings whose annual "earnings" from their organizations average more than one hundred times their average worker's earnings should seek help; help from professionals, psychiatrists, and clowns and priests if any are available. They need to know whether they are suffering from the kings' diseases of hubris, greed, and runaway egos. Once their diseases are diagnosed, corrective action can be prescribed.

This is also foolish, because few if any kings would do it. To the few who do it, high praise! But for the rest, a much slower process is required, one that gradually inserts priests and clowns into the organizational system. The need is for better balance among the roles played in all of our organizational systems.

Priests and Clowns

Chapter 7 outlined the need to strengthen the presence and influence of our organizational priests and clowns. Put simply, we should encourage our clowns and priests, help them as they play their roles, and offer them some protection, some measure of job security, where possible. Find and offer more uses for these two balancing roles, for example on task forces, committees, and staff organizations such as human resources. This is the basic recommendation of this book.

How does a manager offer protection to clowns and priests when they manage to irritate someone at high level elsewhere in the organization—or irritate the manager himself? One example is for the manager to hand to the offending priest or clown a copy of the letter or e-mail message describing the complaint and say, "Please prepare a reply for me to sign." Another method is to have a thorough discussion about the offense with the priest or clown.

Some tribal cultures have made these roles sacred, that is, of religious importance, and actually provide physical protection. That may be more than is needed here. Here we have serious people playing needed roles who occasionally acquire the label of "corporate irritant." A bit of kingly assistance and understanding is usually all that is needed to provide protection.

Talk about It

It's easy to suggest that change is needed, but it is much more difficult to influence an organization's leaders to actually make changes. We have provided some advice on how to begin. First, try to identify people playing priest and clown roles. Have a talk with them. Find out what they think needs changing and out what frustrates them. The key word here is *talk*. Family members talk with each other. Organization members learn from each other by talking and listening. Talking with others in the organization in order to learn about it is a practice as old as the human race. When the tribe's hunt for a wild animal was over, what did the hunters do? They organized a get-together so that while the animal was being roasted, the hunters could describe their experiences for everyone else. From young to old, everyone lived his or her version of the experience.

Some modern firms organize opportunities for this kind of talk. For example, some firms hold project or "post-mortem" reviews when a project is completed. These reviews are good opportunities for award presentations or successes to be recognized. If the organization is run mostly as a bureaucracy, these meetings tend to be top-down affairs, with managers doing the talking and the workers listening. If the organization allows a bit of informality, or a family style, such reviews become opportunities not only for progress reports but also for everyone to learn. Questions may be asked, and the younger, or newer, members can learn from the problems and successes of the more experienced workers.

A meal is often important in such affairs. Much can be accomplished around a lunch or dinner table in the informal setting provided. Again, what's happening is talking, and the meal makes it somewhat of a family affair. Perhaps the famous business lunches in France are more important than ever. The same is true of the famous Japanese "informal discussions."

Organizations are like families.
Both have their best discussions over a meal.

Few, if any, problems in today's organizations will be solved by the stories and descriptions in this book. However, if we can see more clearly what our organizations are and what roles are being played in them, we can find ideas for improvement. Now that we have names for these four roles, we can use them to help us make some recommendations for our organizations and those who decide things about them. For that to happen, please set yourself the task of becoming an amateur anthropologist. Study your own corporate culture and draw your own conclusions. Then do your part to improve your organization. The way to go about this is to talk about it. Talk about some of the examples in this book. Talk to your priests and clowns once you have identified them. They will enjoy talking about the issues with you. Talk about your organization becoming more family oriented. Encourage more informal, family-style meetings. Talk about the organization and what it "feels" like from the inside. Talk about what might make the work more fun, and therefore probably more productive.

Bibliography

Barzun, Jacques. *From Dawn to Decadence: 500 Years of Western Cultural Life, 1500 to the present.* New York: HarperCollins Publishers, 2000.

Deal, Terrence E., and Allen E. Kennedy. *Corporate Cultures: The Rites and Rituals of Corporate Life.* Reading: Addison-Wesley Publishing Company, 1982.

Greiner, Larry E. "Evolution and Revolution as Organizations Grow," *Harvard Business Review*, May-June 1998.

Howard, Philip K. *The Death of Common Sense: How Law Is Suffocating America.* New York: Warner Books, 1994.

Jay, Antony. *Management and Machiavelli: An Inquiry into the Politics of Corporate Life.* New York: Holt, Rinehart, and Winston, 1967.

Kets de Vries, Manfred F. R. *Leaders, Fools and Impostors: Essays on the Psychology of Leadership.* Lincoln: iUniverse, Inc., 2003.

Kets de Vries, Manfred F. R.: *Life and Death in the Executive Fast Lane.* San Francisco: Jossey-Bass Publishers, 1995.

Machiavelli, Niccolo. *The Prince.* London: The Folio Society, 1970.

Marshall, John. *The Hunters*, documentary film, 1957.

Mintzberg, Henry. *Structure in Fives: Designing Effective Organizations.* Englewood Cliffs: Prentice Hall, 1993.

Ouchi, William G. "Markets, Bureaucracies, and Clans," *Administrative Science Quarterly 25*, (March 1980).

Romine, Ben. *From Stone Age Bands to Modern Leadership: A New Way to Look at Organizations.* Unpublished paper. Charlotte, North Carolina, 1986.

Ruby, Jay, ed. *The Cinema of John Marshall.* Langhorne: Haywood Academic, 1993.

Semler, Ricardo: *Maverick: The Success Story behind the World's Most Unusual Workplace.* New York: Warner Books, 1993.

Thompson, William Irwin. *At the Edge of History: Speculations on the Transformation of Culture.* New York: Harper and Row Publishers, 1971.

Weimer, William A. *Masters and Patrons: Renaissance Solutions for Today's Productivity Problems.* Marietta: Dogwood Publishing Company, 1992.

Weimer, William A. *Learning to Manage in a Complex Organization.* Enschede, the Netherlands: Twente University Press, 1999.

About the Author

William A. Weimer was born in 1934 in Freeport, Illinois. He received a Bachelor of Science degree in physics from Purdue University in 1956. He then joined IBM, where he worked until the end of 1989. His work included positions in sales, systems engineering, human resources, product development, and education and training. He held management positions in each of these areas. Beginning in 1990, Bill worked as an independent lecturer and consultant for university business schools and industrial companies. For two years beginning in 1992, he was president of EuroPACE, a nonprofit firm providing technical and management education throughout Europe by satellite television. At the end of that assignment, he returned to his consulting activities for an additional six years.

Bill is an observer of the corporate organizational scene. Although not trained as an anthropologist, he has played clown and priest roles in corporations for many years. He has been labeled a corporate irritant, and worse. He has written two books and several papers on industrial training and his observations on how our organizations work —or fail to work.

He is now retired. He and his wife, Julie, live in Asheville, North Carolina.

978-0-595-36868-6
0-595-36868-9